FINDING PHIL

FINDING PHIL
Lost in War and Silence

PAUL LEVY

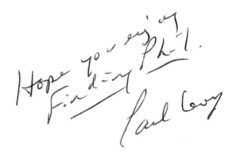

BAUHAN PUBLISHING
PETERBOROUGH, NEW HAMPSHIRE
2016

ISBN: 978-0-87233-224-9

Library of Congress Cataloging-in-Publication Data

Names: Levy, Paul A., 1943-
Title: Finding Phil : lost in war and silence / Paul A. Levy.

Description: Peterborough, New Hampshire : Bauhan Publishing, 2016. |
Includes bibliographical references.
Identifiers: LCCN 2015050632 | ISBN 9780872332249 (paperback :
alkaline paper) Subjects: LCSH: Levy, Phil, 1922-1945. | United States.
Army. Tank Battalion,
191st. | Soldiers—United States—Biography. | Jewish soldiers—United
States—Biography. | World War, 1939-1945—France--Biography. | World
War, 1939-1945—Tank warfare.| Uncles—United States—Biography. | Levy,
Paul A., 1943—Family. | Grief—United States. | Silence—Psychological
aspects.
Classification: LCC D769.306 191st .L38 2016 | DDC 940.54/1273092--
dc23 LC record available at http://lccn.loc.gov/2015050632

Book design by Kirsty Anderson and Sarah Bauhan
Cover design by Henry James.

BAUHAN
PUBLISHING LLC
PO BOX 117 / 44 MAIN STREET PETERBOROUGH NEW HAMPSHIRE 03458
603-567-4430
WWW.BAUHANPUBLISHING.COM

CONTENTS

Prologue: The Sound of Silence   7

MY SEARCH BEGINS

1. The Package   11
2. Into the Vosges   17

YOUTH

3. Introducing Phil   25
4. The Choice   33
5. Barbara   45

WAR

6. Aboard the *Dunera*   57
7. An Irony of Phil on the *Dunera*   71
8. Did Galula Make It Through?   77
9. Into Combat   84
10. At the Front   99
11. Mystery at the Border   112
12. To the End   119
13. And Beyond   129
14. Nuremberg, Zoepf, and Voss   142

GIVING MEANING

15. Louis   158
16. Nathan   166
17 Mark   177
18. Return to Petit Wingen   182
19. Return to Wingen-sur-Moder   192

Epilogue: Stories and Silences   204
Notes   211
Selected Bibliography   218
Map and Photograph Credits   220
Acknowledgments   222

Prologue

The Sound of Silence

Most war stories are untold. Returning soldiers often bury them under grief or guilt, to shield loved ones from horrors they witnessed, or simply in a fervent and sometimes frenzied effort to regain a modicum of peace and resume their prewar life.

Even the stories that are told are often no more than a step removed from this silence. A friend of mine was about five years old when her family fled to Nazi Germany from Estonia in 1939 to save themselves from the invading Russians. Her grandfather was promptly drafted into the German Army. As a teenager after the war, she asked, "Grandpa, what did you do in the war?" He responded with a three-word story, barely a murmur above his silence, "Many horrible things."

The reluctance to speak is apparent even in professional storytellers like Kurt Vonnegut. It took him twenty-five years after World War II to break his silence in *Slaughterhouse Five*; even then, he could tell his story only through a thinly cloaked alter ego named Billy Pilgrim who had gone crazy in the war.

Likewise with the great German novelist Günter Grass: He survived World War II and became the struggling conscience of the German generation implicated in that era's round of human atrocities. Yet it wasn't until 2006 when he was seventy-nine years old, an acclaimed literary voice, and recipient of the Nobel Prize for Literature, that he finally was able to reveal his story. He had been in the Waffen-SS, Hitler's Special Forces that were condemned collectively as a criminal group at Nuremberg. *Peeling the Onion* describes his sixty-year struggle to understand that piece of his identity.

With soldiers who don't return, the silence is even more pervasive.

Not only are their war stories untold, their pre-war stories are buried as well, and this at the hands of those closest to them. For fear of opening floodgates of their own grief or that of others around them, parents, spouses, siblings, and friends suppress the youthful stories of the boy who eventually marched away. Especially at first, sustaining silence is a challenge. Memories erupt unexpectedly, easily, often—a train whistle, a picture at the back of a drawer, a word in a song, a youth in uniform passing by on the street, the sound of a drum, a certain smell, a certain smile.

Over time, however, silence becomes easier and eventually habitual. It reverberates across and then down the generations. In the end it leaves a nearly anonymous leaf to hang on the family tree. This was the case with my Uncle Phil for both generations immediately above me on that tree. They must have thought about him often, but they kept their stories to themselves. And the inheritance of my generation became Phil's leaf with its skeletal story, "1922–1945, Killed in Action."

Yet sometimes with survivors, or with the families of those lost, the silence that could never be broken must finally, near the end, be broken. So it was with Karyn Driessen's dad who, like Phil, was in the 191st Tank Battalion. Late in life, he allowed his daughters to interview him on a tape I was privileged to hear. So it was with Johann Voss and Wolf Zoepf, two members of the Waffen-SS whom you'll meet later in this book.

And so it was with Phil's still-grieving widow somewhere near the end of her own life. She decided to allow a few relics of her long silence to be shared upon her death—a few fragments of her husband's story, of their story. Certainly she knew the recipient would cherish those story fragments; perhaps she also secretly hoped he might be enticed by those fragments to become a storyteller himself. I was the recipient of those relics.

My Search Begins

I

The Package

I have often thought of keeping a journal

I was a year old when Phil died—killed in a tank in World War II, somewhere in France. His final face to the world tells us that he was:

Lt. Phillip A. Levy
March 7, 1922
January 7, 1945
Killed in Action

Lt. Levy was "Uncle Phil" to me, but I grew up learning little more about him than his gravestone revealed. Like many families devastated by the loss of a boy in the war, my family rarely spoke of Phil and my sense of him and his life was embodied in only a few scattered facts. I had heard, for example, that he was a skilled drummer, that he had attended the University of Michigan like most of my family, and that his best friend at college was Mark Van Aken.

Of course I also knew that Phil had married Barbara, and my research revealed that their wedding took place only three or four days before Phil left for North Africa.

After the war, Barbara remarried and settled in her hometown of Indianapolis. Occasionally she visited my parents in South Bend, and I recall those visits as short and generally somber. She sat and talked with my parents while my sister and I went out to play. From those visits, we knew that Barbara was somehow very special to our parents so she was very special to us as well, but she was nearly as much a mystery as our Uncle Phil.

With one important exception, I had little contact with Barbara after I left home, and particularly after my parents died in the early 1970s. So I didn't know that Barbara had died in 1987 until I received a package later that year from an unknown sender. The note inside stated:

> I am sending Phil's diary and Purple Heart to you for Gil. He is recovering from lower back disc surgery. . . . He seems to think he told you he would send this to you. . . .
> Marjorie Cohn (Barbara's sister)

Phil's Purple Heart, front and back

I knew nothing of Barbara's birth family so I had never heard of Marjorie Cohn, but I knew that Gil was Gil Fischbach, Barbara's third husband. My wife and I had dinner with them in the late 1970s in Indianapolis. Gil was very pleasant, Barbara seemed quite happy, and we all talked about our then-current lives. But there was no mention of Phil, no promise to send me a package some day, and no mention of a Purple Heart or a journal. Nor did Barbara and I talk about Phil when we met a short time later to continue our conversation. I can only guess that Barbara told Gil she wanted me to have the items in the package when she died. I suspect that arranging to send these relics to me was the only way Barbara could reveal a little about Phil without violating the family's impulse toward silence.

The package arrived when I was busy with life. I glanced at the Purple Heart and the several pictures and letters in the package, skimmed the journal, and then set the package on a shelf, promising that I would attend to it more carefully when I had time. It would be quite a while before I would translate that intention into action.

In this, apparently, I was a bit like my uncle. He began his journal this way:

9 August, 1944 Wed.
Aboard the British Trooper "Dunera"

> During these past months, I have often thought of keeping a diary or journal, but this thought has never been translated into action—and this for a number of reasons. I suppose that the fact that I once read that only introverts kept diaries has frightened me. No doubt some fears on the question of military security have kept me from undertaking such enterprise. I have been able to confide in my beloved wife to such an extent that all my experiences and thoughts have been recorded in my letters to her. But I prefer to believe that all of these considerations have been far overshadowed by my own, innate laziness which has kept me from ever, until now, starting such a journal and which, I have no doubt of it, will lead this work to a speedy termination.

Phil was right about a speedy termination for he ended the journal after only eighteen daily entries. But he was wrong about the cause. It certainly wasn't his laziness. Journaling requires a particular type of time—time without major diversions, clumps of time that allow for reflection about such things as one's own introversion or one's laziness or one's beloved wife. And war rarely offers much time of this sort. However, for one brief period during the war, Phil had time for reflection. For a week he was aboard the HMT *Dunera* that was

First page of Phil's journal

part of a fleet sailing from Naples, Italy, to the southern coast of France to begin an important campaign called Operation Dragoon. For that week, Phil had few responsibilities and he handwrote most of his ninety-six-page journal during this time.

To attend to the journal and reflect upon my uncle required the same sort of reflective time that Phil had needed, and I didn't get a moment like that in my life until I retired. Getting to Phil and his journal was among my retirement priorities, and so I began my search in earnest early in 2011. I realized that my quest to get to know Phil might result, at best, in a very sketchy portrait at this distant date. I had little hope of finding many additional sources beyond the few I had—about a dozen letters Phil had written to my parents and other family members; some recollections of Jean, Phil's youngest sister and his only surviving sibling; and, of course, the journal.

I began my search by reading the journal. It probably had four readers. The first, as revealed by occasional red or black slashes and the word "delete" here and there, was some anonymous army censor. Barbara read it, probably some parts over and over, certainly sobbing. Phil's youngest sister never saw the journal, and I doubt that either his older sister or his parents saw it or would have wanted to read it. I think they would have sensed that it would only compound their grief.

On the other hand, I suspect that Nathan, Phil's older brother and my father, read the journal, for he would not have let his grief deprive him of a last communication with his beloved younger brother. Later, another surprise package, as important to me as the one containing Phil's journal, would confirm that Nathan indeed had read it. He, like Barbara, would have read it through tears, for my dad's deepest emotions, both elation and grief, inevitably surfaced through tears, a trait that I inherited.

So I was the journal's fourth reader. I cried at times as I read it, touched by Phil's sensitivity and earnestness, his honesty, humanity, naïveté, and humor. But, unlike Barbara and Nathan, I was reading to discover Phil, not to mourn him. It would be some months before I, too, would mourn him each time I revisited his journal.

Discovery at that point simply meant an effort to find a few Phil stories that could replace the anonymous hyphen that filled the space between 1922 and 1945 on Phil's grave and beneath his leaf on the family tree. I organized my quest through questions: What did Phil do in his South Bend boyhood? How did he decide to be a soldier? Who was Barbara and how did she and Phil meet? What did Phil do in the army? Were there ways other than silence that my family used to deal with their grief? Did Phil share Nathan's commitment to social justice? Eventually I found many more stories about Phil than I imagined possible, enough to feel that I had come to know him pretty well and to love him a great deal.

But as I searched to learn about Phil's life, a funny thing happened. My search began to take on a life of its own. It began to produce both Phil stories and Paul adventures. Some of my adventures involved learning new things such as Allied strategies in the European Theater so that I could track Phil during the war, and how the army handles its dead. Others led me to discover new things about my ancestry and my family. Yet other adventures led me to self-reflect, to explore my sense of "heroism," for example, or my stereotype of Nazis.

At times searches lured me onto off-ramps that sometimes led to cul-de-sacs and dead ends, but often to interesting places like Oceanside, New York; Sejny, Russia; and Lembach, France; as well as to unexpected people who may be familiar to you, like Gene Krupa, General David Petraeus, and Kurt Vonnegut, and to others who may be unfamiliar, like Linda and Jacky Bergmann from the Alsace region of France, a French soldier named Galula, and a German soldier from Latvia named Zoepf.

As I said, I framed my search with questions, and initially one question dominated my interest and research: Where did Phil die? I knew only that he had died "somewhere in France."

2

Into the Vosges

Somewhere in France

I knew that Phil was killed in France on January 7, 1945, but had no idea where and had few clues to help me. I knew from his journal that he participated in the invasion of southern France on August 16, 1944, and that he had reported for duty with the 191st Tank Battalion on October 15 of that year after serving behind the lines. An article enclosed in one of Phil's last letters home indicated that he had crossed from France into Germany on December 15, 1944, but none of his other wartime letters in my possession mentioned his location, and such references usually would have been deleted by military censors had he included them.

I figured the best way to pinpoint Phil's location when he died was to follow general troop movements of the Allies in Europe. Very quickly I found that the invasion of southern France was the start of Operation Dragoon. Just as quickly, I realized that I would need at least a working knowledge of World War II to follow troop movements, so I gave myself a crash course in the war before trying to track my uncle across France. Let me summarize some key knowledge I gained in case your memory of that war is as cloudy as mine was.

World War II—101

America was a late entrant into the War. By the time we declared war, the conflict was more than two years old and Germany occupied almost all of Europe, including most nations that thought they could avoid occupation by neutrality agreements. Moreover, Japan had begun its sweep through the Pacific and had devastated the major threat to that sweep, the US Navy's Pacific fleet at Pearl Harbor in Hawaii.

We were unprepared for war. Through the Lend-Lease program, we had provided the Allies with significant amounts of supplies and equipment, but we were not at all war-ready. Our stock of armaments—planes, tanks, ships, guns, etc.—was depleted and badly outdated. Our troops were sparse and untrained. We needed to retool our industries for war production, design and build reliable weapons, and recruit and train an adequate armed force. Congress, hopeful that the war in Europe would be fought only by Europeans, failed to approve most of these activities and appropriate funds necessary to carry them out until their hand was forced on December 7, 1941, by Pearl Harbor.

Our late entry and unpreparedness dictated our war strategy— retreat to victory. We needed time to produce troops and arms that could confront Axis powers on equal terms, and the only way to buy that time was to adopt a strategy called, by at least one author, a "retreat to victory."[1] We would reluctantly cede locations in the Pacific and help England and Russia only with supplies and equipment and only from a distance, tolerating German and Japanese advances while trying to make their victories as costly to them as possible. At the same time we would build our own war capacity at a record pace so that we could enter the fray offensively. This defensive posture was expected to last at least a year and a half or two years.

The shift from defensive retreat to offensive attack began in the winter of 1942–43. In the Pacific Theater, this shift began at Guadalcanal. In the European Theater, it began with a push to conquer North Africa and establish a base for invading continental Europe. After conquering North Africa and then Sicily, the island at the toe of Italy, the invasion of the continent began on September 9, 1943, with landings at Salerno, Italy. All of this happened before Uncle Phil arrived in Europe. At that point the Allies envisioned the long-anticipated liberation of France and the rest of occupied Europe, and the final advance toward Berlin. General Eisenhower was named Supreme Allied Commander in early 1944 to plan that assault.

The Allied strategy for invading and liberating Europe consisted of two major initiatives: a landing in northern France at Normandy called Operation Overlord, which was carried out by a mix of Allied forces known as the Twelfth Army Group; and a landing in southern France called Operation Dragoon, which was carried out by Allied forces known as the Sixth Army Group, composed essentially of the US Seventh Army and the French First Army. Overlord began on June 6, 1944 (D-Day), and Dragoon began on August 15. The plan was for the Overlord troops to move south, the Dragoon troops to move north, and the two to meet and form a single north-south line that could then move east liberating France, Belgium, the Netherlands, and other German-occupied territory, cross the borders into Germany, move toward Berlin, and end the war. Winston Churchill, Prime Minister of England, opposed the southern (Dragoon) component of this strategy, feeling that it would spread Allied troops too thin, but General Eisenhower, with his two-pronged strategy, prevailed.

The shift from defense to offense and then to liberation meant sharp rises in casualties. In the defensive or retreat phase of American strategy, we tried to stay out of harm's way to preserve our troops to the extent possible, helping allies with supplies and equipment while building our own capacity. In Europe, much of our early support was given to the air war, which had its own casualties but not nearly as severe as those in the ground war. As we invaded the mainland, Allied casualties immediately skyrocketed. This, of course, was true for Germany as well, and both sides became increasingly challenged by the need to find fresh troops for the front to replace those wounded, captured, or killed.

My Search Begins

During my crash course, I learned that there were various types of military records, both personal and unit records, and how to request them. I sent for Phil's personnel records housed at the Military's National Personnel Records Center in St. Louis, and for daily records of the 191st Tank Battalion for the week Phil died, which were housed at the National Archives in College Park, Maryland. While awaiting those records, I began to track troop movements from Phil's landing on the French Riviera in Operation Dragoon.

In great contrast to the Overlord troops invading at Normandy, the Dragoon troops met relatively little German resistance on the beaches of the French Riviera. They landed and were able to fight their way quickly northward up the Rhône River Valley. By early September, they had turned eastward and were in the vicinity of Lyon, France. Meanwhile, the Normandy troops had moved much more slowly. They had secured their position in Normandy after taking heavy losses, and then in July began to move south (in what was called Operation Breakout) and by July 25 began the next phase (Operation Cobra) in which they moved east to Paris. After liberating Paris on August 25, the Normandy troops continued eastward.

On September 11 the Dragoon and Normandy troops made contact, forming a rough but continuous north-south line that began to move east toward the German border. The Allied armies in the northern and southern portions of the line remained distinct. They encountered different terrains and variations in German resistance, and as a result moved at quite different paces. By December, both were nearing the German border, but neither would begin the march across Germany to victory until the spring of 1945.

Phil was involved in the southern invasion and was part of the Sixth Army Group. By the time he joined the 191st Tank Battalion in mid-October, the Group had reached the Vosges Mountains in France somewhere near Épinal, the future site of the American Cemetery that would be the final resting place of most Americans killed in action in this sector of the war.

The Vosges Mountains run north and south, forming the western wall of the Rhine River Valley. They form two sections, the High Vosges to the south and the Low Vosges to the north that end just over the border into Germany. The 191st along with the rest of the Sixth Army Group remained in the Vosges until two months after Phil was killed. So, through this initial research, I had identified the vicinity where Phil's life ended. It also turned out to be the vicinity of

Operation Dragoon, August 1944

the chief achievement in his military career and a highlight of his short life. Seventy years later, these same mountains were the area where my search for Phil essentially ended and where I, too, experienced a great highlight of life.

But as a storyteller, I have gotten far ahead of my story. There is much territory covered in both Phil's life and my adventure before either of us ascended the Vosges Mountains. And worse, I have been a rude host, for I have not yet even introduced you to my uncle.

Youth

Phil as a senior at the University of Michigan

3

Introducing Phil

And making us like it

Phil was born in 1922, the fourth of Louis and Bessie Levy's five children. He grew up in South Bend, Indiana, where his father, in 1896 at age sixteen, had emigrated from Russia. Louis became a peddler pushing a cart around the county, saved enough money to bring the rest of his family to South Bend, and eventually became a modest Horatio Alger: pushcart to horse-drawn cart, to truck, to successful company—Levy-Ward Wholesale Fruit and Vegetable Company. The family lived alongside immigrants from many countries and numbers of African Americans from the South who supplied much of the labor for the city's burgeoning industries, notably: Studebaker Wagon Company that became the automobile company (the only American wagon company to successfully make this transition); the Oliver Chilled Plow Company, which played a prominent role in the industrialization of American agriculture; and the Singer Sewing Machine Company, which set up its primary cabinet-making operation in South Bend.

As Phil moved into school, he had big shoes to fill. Nathan was Louis and Bessie's oldest child, thirteen years older than Phil. He was also the first first-generation (American-born) Levy in the extended family. In these positions, Nathan not only felt driven to assimilate but also driven to excel, and he managed these responsibilities unbelievably well. He was the first Levy to attend high school, and he was a stellar student. Not only did he become competent in English, he became a state champion high school orator. A special page was

LEE DOUGLAS
Announcer.

Lee Douglas (Nathan) at WSBT Radio,
about 1940

Louis and Bessie, 1946

devoted to him in his high school yearbook in 1927. With his picture at the top, the lengthy article below it began, "No student has brought more fame to South Bend High or has gained greater recognition for himself than Nathan Levy."

Nathan was the first Levy to attend college, and he went to a fine school, the University of Michigan, known at the time as the "Harvard of the West." (He had no interest in applying to Harvard after hearing that it maintained quotas on Jews.) Not only did he attend Michigan, but he excelled as a student there, was a champion debater, and was president of various oratorical clubs. Not only was Nathan the first Levy to graduate from college, but he was also the first to attend professional school—the prestigious law school of the University of Michigan—where, again, he excelled. He graduated third in his class, and one law professor called him "a born lawyer" and "the most likely eventually to succeed of any man in [his] class."

Louis and Nathan, about 1950

Nathan struggled to start a law practice in South Bend—it was the Depression—and would eventually become City Attorney and soon after join an old, respected South Bend law firm as its first Jew. While struggling, he supplemented his income by announcing Notre Dame football games for the local radio station and hosting a very popular early morning show, *The Morning Bugle*. Because lawyers couldn't advertise in those days, Nathan used the alias Lee Douglas. Recently a Notre Dame alumnus included this item on a list of his school-day highlights: "WSBT and the irrepressible wake-up voice of Lee Douglas."[2] And finally, Nathan was the first of the siblings to marry, to own a home, and to have children.

Quite a resumé, and Phil was intimidated. In a wartime letter to his younger sister who was struggling academically as a freshman at Michigan, Phil counseled, "Don't let the Big Brain's record (. . . yes I mean the Sage of LaSalle Street) bother you." But intimidation hardly dominated Phil's relationship with his big brother; instead Nathan was the amenable mentor and Phil the adoring mentee, and, given the thirteen years between them, they were surprisingly close friends.

Phil—smart, inquisitive, literate, and a critical thinker with a broad array of interests quite similar to Nathan's—not only managed to follow in Nathan's footsteps but to create notable footsteps of his own. Like Nathan, Phil was a fine student in high school and went on to the University of Michigan where he did well. Phil also became a debater, served as president of his high school debate club and, though not a state champion, was good enough to be on the University of Michigan's debate team as well.

In another important respect, Phil seemed to follow Nathan. Louis and Bessie were Orthodox Jews, keeping kosher, observing the Sabbath, and so forth. As an adult and perhaps earlier, Nathan began to distance himself from formal religious practices while holding onto his strong Jewish cultural identity. Often, for example, he told old Jewish stories or drew upon ancient Jewish ethical traditions in making a point. Eventually he and his wife, Norma, belonged to the Reform Temple in town and were very good friends with its rabbi and his wife, but they rarely attended services. Instead, as Jews, they committed themselves to reducing barriers of religion, race, and class, and promoting the commonality of people across those lines. I think Phil shared these views. He was not in a Jewish fraternity at college, for example, or active in Hillel (an organization for Jewish students at Michigan and many other campuses), or active in a synagogue or temple.

But by no means was Phil simply a disciple of Nathan. In major ways, he shaped his own path. One of these was with music. After taking piano lessons at an early age, he became very interested in music. The piano led to various other instruments such as the glockenspiel and bugle, and eventually the drums. In high school he organized a jazz band that practiced in his garage and played at various South Bend events. Then, in college, he organized another jazz band that played in sororities, fraternities, and other local venues.

One of the few bits of Phil lore I heard in my childhood was that he had been a finalist in a drumming contest in Chicago, came in third,

Phil as a young boy

and played for some moments with the legendary Gene Krupa. My research indicated that this contest was probably the one held in 1940 by the premier drum manufacturer Slingerland Drum Company, headquartered in Chicago and with Mr. Krupa as its celebrity spokesman. The contest was national, drew over forty thousand contestants, and was won by seventeen-year-old Louie Bellson who later became a hall of fame drummer performing with the Dorseys, Duke Ellington, Harry James, and all the greats. Bellson's victory was in the finals in New York City,[3] but since he was from Moline, Illinois, he would have competed in the Chicago regional, so it is likely that Phil came in third to Bellson—which suggests that Phil was probably pretty talented.

In high school, Phil also became deeply interested in student government. He served on the Student Council as its president, vice president, and secretary in various years. He also was president of the Band and the Forensics Club. In his senior year Phil became president of the Indiana Association of Student Councils (IASC), which was comprised of representatives from other student councils in Indiana. The quote under Phil's picture in his Senior Yearbook is, "Governing Indiana and making us like it." Apparently his fellow students imagined a political future for Phil.

I hadn't expected to learn even this much about Phil's youth, sixty-five years after his death, but the more I learned about what he did, the more I wondered who he was. I wanted to get more of a sense of his character—his motivations, temperament, spirit, passions, dreams, morality. . . . I began to wonder, for example, whether he

Phil in his early teens

was deeply committed to social justice like Nathan and Norma. Various comments in his letters to Nathan and particularly in his journal suggested a similar commitment. For example, aboard the HMT *Dunera*, the British ship that carried Phil and higher-level officers to the invasion of southern France, Phil was bothered that all the waiters were Indian, described their demeanor, and wrote about how an independent India had to be an immediate post-war priority of England and the world.

A particularly interesting indicator of Phil's commitment to justice turned out to be the jazz band he organized in high school—the one that practiced in the Levy garage and ate sandwiches prepared by Bessie, Phil's mom. The band was predominantly African American. An integrated band in Indiana in the 1930s was unusual. Indeed it would have been unusual in most places in the United States at the time, but certainly in a state that had been home to the resurgence of the KKK in the 1920s—home to the largest Klan gathering ever, in Kokomo, Indiana, in 1924; home to KKK marches including in South Bend in 1924;[4] and home to a governor and a majority of legislators who belonged to the Klan until that government was ousted in 1926. Of course, there was much opposition in the state to the racist, antisemitic, and anti-Catholic Klan, including in South Bend with its major Catholic university and substantial Catholic immigrant population.

I happened to hear a recording of John Cougar Mellencamp speaking before he sang "Eyes on the Prize" at a Martin Luther King Day celebration in 2010 at the White House. He talked about his

Phil in high school

rebellious youth, which included forming an "interracial band, in Indiana, in 1966!"[5] In an earlier interview he recalled that, at that time, his hometown of Seymour, Indiana, "still had signs reading, 'Black man, don't let the sun set on you here.'" The fact that the band antagonized the town elite only added to the commitment of fourteen-year-old Mellencamp. Seymour and South Bend were quite different towns in the 1930s and in the 1960s. Seymour had few blacks and much more of a southern racial influence, and it didn't have a Catholic university or a large Catholic population of immigrants to oppose the Klan. But Mellencamp's daring in 1966 helped me understand that Phil's band, thirty years earlier, was not only playing music but also taking a significant social stand.[6]

The question about Phil's character that began to interest me most, however, was what I began to refer to as The Choice. In September 1939, Phil registered for his freshman year at the University of Michigan and chose an academic program that, upon graduation, would lead to officers' candidate school and then the army. This decision was made only days after Germany invaded Poland on September 1 to start World War II, and over two years before Pearl Harbor led many young men and America itself to join the war. Phil was aware that his decision was exceptional. In a letter late in the war, he told Nathan, "[I] was looking forward to my commission in 1939 when most of my fellows were having Peace Rallies, figuring out how to stop compulsory military service, and the like." Phil was not from a military family, didn't grow up with guns, and didn't seem at all like a warrior at heart. So what, I wondered, prompted his choice?

Phil with the author's sister Gail, about 1942

4

The Choice

My people need me

Phil's choice was not precipitous. He seemed to be deliberate and informed when he shaped opinions and took action, not a surprising trait of someone deeply involved in high school governance and debate or a mentee of Nathan. What helped me most to understand the thinking that led Phil to his choice was to imagine him in the context of his family and in the context of events of his time, the 1920s and '30s.

The Arc

The arc of the Levy family experience ran from Sejny to South Bend. Sejny is the town where Phil's father, Louis, was born in 1880; the town that Louis and his father Moses left when they emigrated in 1896; and the town where the rest of the family remained until, over the course of the next ten years, Moses and Louis could afford to bring them to South Bend. Sejny lies in a swath of land between the Baltic and Black Seas that belonged, at various times over the centuries, to Lithuania, Prussia, Germany, and Russia before becoming part of modern day Poland in 1920.

Between 1791 and 1917, this area was part of Russia and became known as "The Pale of Settlement." In 1791, Catherine the Great became the first ruler to issue decrees exiling Jews to the Pale. In addition, the government sanctioned rampages ("pogroms") throughout Russia, destroying Jewish stores, homes, and synagogues, raping and killing Jews, and driving Jews to the Pale. As a result, the

Pale of Settlement, about 1896

Jewish population in the Pale grew to five million in the late 1800s when Louis emigrated.

Normally life was very hard in the Pale, and intermittently, depending on the czar at the time, it was agonizingly harsh. In *Fiddler on the Roof*, Tevye's village of Anatevka is simply a somewhat chic, fictional, Broadway rendition of Sejny or any of the other small villages in the Pale—and *Fiddler* takes place at about the time Louis lived there. When Louis was born, the regime was relatively humanitarian, but when Czar Alexander II was assassinated in 1881 and Jews were blamed, there was a spate of pogroms—two hundred that year including many within the Pale. In 1882, Czar Alexander III enacted a set of harsh anti-Jewish policies called the May Laws that were broadened over the decade. They restricted places within the

Postcard of Sejny in 1880s

Pale where Jews could settle, for example, and they set harsh quotas on the percentages of Jewish youth who could attend high school (10 percent within the Pale and 5 percent outside). Then in 1891, an edict expelled twenty thousand Jews from Moscow to the Pale, and other Russian cities followed suit.[7]

Many Jews—about three million after the assassination of the Czar—left the Pale to seek a better life. In 1896, Moses, with sixteen-year-old Louis, joined the exodus. Despite the exodus, however, the Jewish population of the Pale grew through in-migrations and a high birth rate. This continued after the area became part of an independent Poland following World War I. Germany invaded Poland in 1939, and by war's end, almost all of Poland's three million Jews had been killed, many in the six Nazi death camps (Auschwitz, Belzec, Chelmo, Majdanek, Sobibor, and Treblinka). Notably all of these were located in Poland, in or near the area that had been The Pale. Most likely, had Louis and his siblings remained in Sejny, all would have been killed and probably at Treblinka, about a two-hour boxcar ride from Sejny.

South Bend central business district in the 1920s

At the other end of the arc was South Bend. When Louis, Moses, and soon the family arrived, South Bend had a sizeable and growing Jewish community: 125 Jews in 1878 had grown to 1,200 by 1912. Most were German Jews, and at least one history says that they got along well with the large German Christian community in town. The two communities established and oversaw a series of social and service institutions—a German choir, German lodge, and the Turneverein, a gymnastics center.[8]

Other immigrant populations fed the labor needs of the emerging industrial center and most lived on the city's west side where the Levy family settled. In larger cities, nationality groups would have separated into neighborhoods such as the Chicago neighborhoods of Bridgeport (the original Irish area), Germantown, Swedish Andersonville, Polish Village, and Greek Town. In South Bend, however, immigrant groups were more integrated, and all children went to South Bend High School until 1932 when a second high school opened and South Bend High became Central High. So, when Louis married Bessie in 1909 and rented a house on Cushing Street, many of their neighbors were first-generation Americans from an array of nations—Germany, Austria, Sweden, Ireland, and Canada—and their immediate neighbors had such names as Findley, Richardson, Heil, and Kreis, reflecting this array. Growing up, Phil and his brother Nathan had a diverse set of friends that, besides those who were Jewish, included the Rulli brothers (Italian), Eddie Wegenky (Polish), Michael Lochmandy (Hungarian), and Felix Jones (Welsh).

A story from the South Bend end of the arc contrasts the melting pot acceptance and opportunity that Louis and his family found in America with the life they left in the Pale. Garnet Rose Lutes recalled Moses and Louis in a series of articles in a local weekly newspaper in the 1970s. She had been a small girl on the Rose farm near Lakeville, ten miles south of South Bend, when Moses, accompanied by Louis, visited to peddle his wares. They came monthly and "usually arrived at the Rose farm on Friday afternoons and stayed over the weekend." On Saturday, the Jewish Sabbath, they couldn't work and on Sunday, the Christian Sabbath, they couldn't sell their wares. They and the Roses became friends—Moses and Mr. Rose would discuss the Bible on Sunday afternoons; Mrs. Rose, concerned about their visitors' feet, urged them to get a horse for their cart which they did; each new Levy arrival was taken to meet the Roses and Mrs. Rose taught some of them English. "The two families were friends for many years," and the friendship lasted beyond the peddling days and was carried on by the children.[9]

Lutes's articles were included in materials left to my sister and me by our mother. She had typed a cover note explaining the articles and adding that, when Phil was killed, "Mrs. Rose, then very old, infirm, and blind, came with her daughter to pay her respects. She entered the home saying, 'I heard that my friend Louis was in trouble, and I came to help him.'"

Phil and his siblings revered their parents. This is not always the case between first and second generations. The tension that inevitably arises between an immigrating generation, as it keeps a foot in the old country even as it plants a foot in the new one, and a first generation that eagerly plants both feet in the new land in a zealous effort to assimilate, can tear parents and children apart. Certainly the Levy family had such tensions, but still they remained quite close. So I'm confident Phil was aware of the origin and struggles of his parents and had a deep pride in their accomplishments.

The opportunity and acceptance that he and his family experienced left Phil with a great love of his country. Moreover, Phil had seen America progress. He had witnessed, for example, the demise of the Klan's control of Indiana government referred to earlier, and he saw America adopt a New Deal to confront the Depression. Following his brother's lead, Phil was acquiring a deep confidence in American democracy—its rule of law, its process of dialogue and debate—as a force for good. All this added to Phil's patriotic commitment.

This is not to suggest that Phil and his family were oblivious to American problems, including the problem of antisemitism. Eugenics, a pseudo-science that classified people by "race," had become quite popular in America in the early 1900s. It distinguished Nordics or Aryans, the "race" of northern and western Europe, from various races of southern Europe, including Mediterranean races such as Semites. Then it ranked these races. Nordics (Aryans, Anglo-Saxons, Celtics . . .) were ranked as superior—by far the most evolved and advanced—while southern European races were distinctly inferior. Semites were ranked at or near the bottom of the bunch along with Africans. Eugenics mixed race and color, considering non-Nordics to be non-white. Social changes during the century would turn Jews and other non-Nordics "white" in America while leaving Africans black.[10]

At its height in America, Eugenics fed the xenophobia that arose with the heavy immigration at the turn of the century. "Race suicide" is how Teddy Roosevelt described the impact of immigration on America, and other notables such as Charles Lindbergh, Margaret Sanger, and Henry Cabot Lodge agreed. Eugenics not only gave rise to the resurgence of the KKK referred to earlier, but spawned many proposals for preventing racial contamination and for retaining or re-purifying superior gene pools. Most importantly, it led to the Immigration Act of 1924 and its quota system that banned almost all immigrants from eastern and southern Europe as well as from the Orient, India, and Africa. This act was not significantly changed until 1965.

The impact of Eugenics in America began to wane in the 1930s—an example of progress that gave Phil hope. He may not have fully appreciated what history would soon reveal—how deeply Hitler had appropriated this popular American pseudo-science. When Nazi defendants at Nuremberg after the war testified that they had been inspired by Eugenics voices, findings, and policy initiatives coming from the United States, they were speaking most uncomfortable truths.

Current Events

In addition to these lessons from the family arc—from the Pale to America—another powerful force helped shape Phil's choice. He was deeply interested in current events and, by virtue of his debate training, highly skilled in assessing them.

Phil certainly followed the news in newspapers and on the radio, and much of that news concerned events in Europe and reactions in the United States. Some of that news involved German treatment of Jews, and Phil and his family were part of a Jewish community (a largely German Jewish community) that kept up with these events not simply from the media but also from communications with relatives in the old country.

Debate provided Phil with the skills of critical analysis generally, but it also required that he learn and think about events in Europe specifically, for many of the popular debate topics of the late 1930s and early '40s involved these unfolding events. Topics included: whether the United States should declare war on the Axis powers immediately, whether we should join a federation of English-speaking nations to oppose Germany, whether the Lend-Lease Bill should be enacted, whether embargoes against Axis powers were wise, whether the United States should begin to rearm, and, most popular in high schools, whether the United States should reinstate the draft and compulsory military service.[11]

For those not familiar with debating, these introductory comments to a summary of a competition between Oberlin College and Ohio Wesleyan in 1939 provide a sense of the timeliness of debate topics and the level of detail demanded of good debaters. [12] The question posed was whether pro-German organizations in the United States should be repressed:

> This debate was particularly timely as it was held at the eventful moment when the full consequences of "fifth column" activities in Holland and Belgium were following precipitately upon those in Norway and Denmark. Also it was on the day that President Roosevelt made a speech which specifically noticed the danger of such subversive activities in this country. The debate came at a time when bills for suppression or some definite limiting action for subversive activities were being agitated and introduced into Congress. It is not often that academic debaters get a chance at such a pertinent subject at the psychological moment of its greatest public interest.

From the media, the Jewish grapevine, and debate, Phil realized a few things. One was that German antisemitism was escalating rapidly. Perhaps the most dramatic evidence of this was Kristallnacht, when "Nazi storm troopers carried out the infamous pogrom against the Jews of Germany."

> On Nov. 9 and 10, 1938, about 1300–1500 Jews were murdered and 30,000 more were sent to concentration camps. 1574 synagogues were burned down. More than 7,000 Jewish-owned businesses were destroyed. The vast amount of shattered glass from the windows of Jewish homes and shops gave the rampage its name, "Crystal Night," or "Night of the Broken Glass."
> During the previous five years, Germany's Jews had been stripped of their legal rights and subjected to occasional outbursts of violence, but nothing comparable to the systematic, nationwide devastation of Kristallnacht. [13]

Phil also would have been well aware of America's reluctance to help persecuted Jews. He would have understood Kristallnacht as the likely outcome of an event that happened just four months earlier. In July 1938, FDR called thirty-two nations (all eventually joined the Allies in the war or tried to retain neutrality) to a conference in Evian, France, to explore what could be done to help Jews in Germany. Much concern was registered but no country, including the United States, took significant steps to help. This was what Hitler had predicted and he mocked the Evian conferees in a January 1939 speech to the Reichstag soon after Kristallnacht:

> It is a shameful spectacle to see how the whole democratic
> world is oozing sympathy for the poor tormented Jewish
> people, but remains hard-hearted and obdurate when
> it comes to helping them, which is surely, in view of its
> attitude, an obvious duty.[14]

Many see Evian as the "green light" Hitler needed for genocide.

Phil also was very aware that the majority of Americans preferred isolationism, believing that the war in Europe was none of our business. This view was even held by many Jews including influential ones such as Arthur Ochs Sulzberger, publisher of the *New York Times*. According to one commentator on the subject, prior to Pearl Harbor the publisher wanted to avoid any appearance of pleading for special help for Jews for fear of validating the isolationist claim "that Jews would lure America into war [just] to help their persecuted brothers." He also was "particularly eager to be seen as [a] good American adhering to the government line."[15]

Phil realized that FDR believed that the United States would eventually have to become heavily involved in the war and had begun to press for policies in that direction. Some of those initiatives began to be adopted by a reluctant Congress soon after Phil made his 1939 decision; for example, a peacetime draft was approved in 1940, and the Lend-Lease Program was approved in early 1941.

The Choice

So, when Phil registered for freshman courses at the University of Michigan in September 1939, he had a strong Jewish identity, compassion for German and other embattled Jews, and an informed apprehension about the escalation of Nazi antisemitism. He wanted to help Jews: My sister recalls our father (Nathan) relating to us that Phil told him, "My people need me."

He also had a strong and confident American identity and an informed sense of the inevitability of war in Europe and of America's inescapable involvement in that war. Phil wanted to support America as it became embroiled in Europe's problems. He saw preparing to fight as the only way to fulfill these two desires. In college, he would add a third reason to fight. He majored in French and came to love the language and culture of France. So, when France surrendered to Germany on June 22, 1940, Phil acquired yet another justification for preparing for war.

It was a surprise to discover that Phil's strong Jewish and American identity was rare among Jewish boys, especially ones from the East Coast, prior to the war. Many had grown up isolated in Jewish neighborhoods and had their first contacts with gentiles in the army. In an interesting study that looked at East Coast Jews who fought in World War II, Deborah Dash Moore concluded that many Jewish soldiers entered the war with a Jewish identity only to emerge with a Jewish-American identity.[16]

The Choice Plays Out

At Michigan, Phil's program of 121 credits included a military course each term (twelve of the total credits) and thirty credits of French, his major. He also studied Spanish and took a variety of political and European history courses.

Phil graduated in three and a half years, as did many undergraduates during the war years. On Valentines' Day 1943, he reported for active duty at Fort Knox, Kentucky, where the Officers' Candidate School (OCS) specialized in training armored divisions.

ROTC at the University of Michigan; Phil is in the center

The history section of the Fort Knox website describes the OCS program at that time:

> In 1943 [at the Armored Replacement Training Center] .... Here Soldiers received a 17-week course [Phil's was 14 weeks] which included instruction in various arms, big tank guns, tank driving and maintenance, chemical warfare and many other subjects. They were introduced to hills "Misery," "Agony" and "Heartbreak" before graduating and then sent to divisions, additional schooling, or straight into the various theaters of war.[17]

Phil described the harsh details in a letter during his first week there.

Phil in training

There is absolutely no free time here from 5:30 AM to 11
or 12 PM. . . . Wed. we were told to fall out in full field
equipment. They marched us 2 miles most of it double time
to a terrific obstacle course which we had to take with full
equipment—swinging across streams on ropes, scaling walls,
etc. Then we started to march.... Finally, when we were good
and tired, "gas" was sounded and we marched 15 minutes
across country in gas masks—the most horrible experience
you can imagine. It is hard to breathe, you can't talk, and the
sweat fills up the mask.

Thursday there was more marching but Phil's feet were so bad he
couldn't participate. Then, with bandaged feet, he marched on Friday,
returned to eat, went back out to march some more, and ended his
day with three hours of walking Guard.

At Fort Knox, Phil trained as a tank commander. He graduated
as a Second Lieutenant on May 22, 1943, just seventeen days after
I was born. Then he received additional field training, probably at
Fort Benning with the 10th Armored Division. In September, he was
granted a leave and got married on September 12 but was called
back abruptly and left Indiana on September 16 for Atlanta and then
Florida where, soon after, he shipped out to North Africa.

5

Barbara

I woke up to see you coming up the aisle

Before we head toward war with Phil, I want to introduce the love of Phil's life, Barbara Sternfels. She grew up in Indianapolis, Indiana. Barb was a "naturalist," according to her niece, Jane, and loved canoeing, camping, and swimming. She also loved animals, often taking in strays and at one point owning a boa constrictor. Jane contrasted Barbara—"outdoorsy and mild-mannered"—with her older sister (Jane's mother) who was "artistic and aggressive." But the two sisters were close friends. Both attended Indianapolis Shortridge High School and, according to Jane, both sisters were very good looking. In her senior year, Barbara was one of ten finalists to be Shortridge's Bluebelle, a contest that seems similar to selecting a prom queen; Jane thought Barbara might have been the first Jewish finalist.

In high school, Barbara majored in French and history, was an athlete (archery and swimming were her favorite sports), and she also wrote for the Shortridge newspaper, as did her classmate and neighbor, Kurt Vonnegut. Upon graduation in 1940, she enrolled at the University of Michigan, a year after Phil. There she became active in various extracurricular activities—president of Alpha Epsilon Phi, a Jewish sorority, and involved with the university's humor magazine and drama club. After she began to date Phil, she actively participated in the Women's War Council on campus, heading an effort related to St. Joseph Hospital in Ann Arbor.

Barbara also was an excellent student. Like Phil, she moved

BLUEBELLE

Ann Bishop is a remarkable combination of wonderful looks and functioning gray matter. The V-8's boast of her as a member, while the Honor Society claims her more civilized moments. This glorious little gal is the vice-president of the illustrious class of '40 and gave some of the best years of her life to the Student Council of '39.

The class of 1940 proved their superiority in beauty by having two Bluebelles chosen from their class. In 1939, Susan Alvis, now secretary of the class of '40, was crowned.

Other candidates were top, left to right, Barbara Kiger, Pat Failing, Ann Shaw, Mary Ann Morrison, Patty Peterson; center, Bluebelle Ann Bishop; lower, Mary Glossbrenner, Peggy Trusler, '39 Bluebelle, Susan Alvis, Barbara Sternfels, and Marge Geupel.

Bluebelle and contestants at Indianapolis Shortridge High School, 1940. Barbara is at five o'clock.

through school in three and a half years, and became one of twenty-four women in the Class of 1944 selected to The Mortar Board, the Senior Women's Honorary Society, based on her high grades and high level of character and service. After graduation, Barbara became a social worker, practicing on and off the rest of her life, at times working with the Camp Fire Girls and with Crossroads Rehabilitation. After Phil died, Barbara returned to Indianapolis, married her high school boyfriend, Arthur Jacobs, had four children before divorcing, married

Senior pictures of Barbara and classmate Kurt Vonnegut in
the Shortridge High School yearbook

Gil Fischbach in 1975, and died in 1987. My wife and I saw Barb and
Gil a couple of times. He seemed like a very nice guy and Barbara
seemed quite happy. I later read Gil's obituary that mentioned he was
"a World War II veteran, a labor organizer for the Furrier's Union,
and a lifelong fighter for social justice."

Jane recalled a remarkable thing, and I confirmed it. Apparently
Barb and her second husband took vacations in Florida during
winters, and one winter he taught her how to scuba dive. The next
summer she—well, the article from *Sports Illustrated* (February 6,
1956) tells the story:

BARBARA JACOBS
Last winter, while on vacation in Florida, Mr. and Mrs.
Arthur Jacobs of Indianapolis took up Aqua-lung diving. Last
month Barbara Jacobs, a 33-year-old brunette, showed her
husband and two children how proficient she had become by
descending 270 feet into the Atlantic off Hollywood Beach,

Fla. to set the unofficial women's world record. The previous unofficial mark was 209 feet. Assisting Mrs. Jacobs were her husband and Ed Townsend, sectional director of the AAU. Asked what she had noticed on the way down, Mrs. Jacobs reported her red nail polish seemed to turn blue.[18]

A report of this in *The Wilmington* [North Carolina] *News* noted that Barbara "apparently was not bothered by the mysterious 'rapture of the deep' that snuffed out the life of Miami attorney Hope Root when he tried a similar dive off Miami Beach two years ago."[19]

At Michigan, Phil knew Barbara in passing but was too involved with his music, debate, and academic work to date much. Then in 1942 or 1943, they met by chance during a winter break on a train to Miami Beach where they each had vacationing relatives. Phil recalled that meeting in an entry he made in his journal the night before the invasion of southern France.

He was excited—he felt the invasion would be the straw that would break the Germans. He also was scared—I don't think he had been in combat before, and in any event, he knew of the heavy losses at Normandy two months earlier and the dangers of such landings. His entry doesn't refer to either his excitement or fear, but I suspect this mix of emotions is what led him to anticipate a sleepless night. He tells Barbara that he always has had trouble sleeping the night before big events like a debate or a trip to Chicago as a child or even a Boy Scout test, and then he continues:

> I don't recall telling you this before . . . but the night before
> I was to go to Miami Beach was the most sleepless night
> I've ever spent. I boarded the N. Y. Central for Chicago. I
> snoozed a bit on the train and then on the "South Wind."
> It was then that I woke up to see you coming up the aisle
> toward me. And that's a long story. But a very lovely one
> because it's about the loveliest person in the world, the one I
> love beyond all expression.

My research[20] helped me envision the event. The *South Wind* was a new member of the Pennsylvania Railroad fleet. It was painted Tuscan red rather than the more flashy stainless steel preferred by its builder, and it consisted of seven cars—four coaches (and no sleepers), a diner, an observation car, and a baggage car with some coach capacity for blacks since the train ran through southern states that required segregation.

Phil had to get to the South Bend train station very early in order to be in Chicago, ninety miles away, by 8:40 a.m. when the *South Wind* was due to depart. The South Wind's first stop was thirteen minutes out of Chicago, but it didn't stop again until it reached Indianapolis at 12:02 p.m. That allowed Phil a long nap before the screech of brakes awoke him in Indianapolis. He probably was still a bit bleary eyed at 12:05 p.m. when the train pulled out of Indianapolis and Barbara came down the aisle.

After Indianapolis, the South Wind passed through Nashville, Birmingham, Montgomery, Jacksonville, and other towns on its 1,559-mile journey before arriving in Miami Beach at 2:40 the next afternoon. Apparently that provided ample time for Phil and Barb not only to talk but to fall in love.

The *South Wind* leaving Indianapolis

Phil and Barbara at a college dance or graduation party

Phil was head-over-heels in love with Barbara, and Barbara's niece tells me that Barbara felt the same about Phil. So, at the age of twenty-one—she just barely and he for a half-year—while he was on leave following his training and before shipping out to North Africa, they decided to get married. The wedding was in Indianapolis on September 12, 1943, just three or four days before he was unexpectedly called back early from his leave.

I'd like to think that Phil and Barbara were ready for marriage, and I think they probably were. Both were very serious and goal-oriented, neither seemed impulsive, and apparently they were very much in love. But they may have been more like so many wartime couples who marry just as Johnny marches off: Johnny desperate for someone to return to and worried sick that his girlfriend will find someone else while he is gone; the girlfriend feeling too sorry for Johnny to turn him down; so, they get married and off Johnny goes. Of course some of these last-minute marriages last but many don't, and many others end as this one would, with a young widow who must figure out how to get on with her life.

Phil agonized over the marriage decision as he left to embark. In a letter to Nathan sent just eight days after the marriage, Phil shared some feelings and made a request:

> September 20, 1943 (Augusta, Georgia)
> Dear Nate,
>
> . . . I talked to Barb this morning and naturally I was glad to hear that she didn't feel badly about having gotten married. I told her that I was happy about it but naturally I feel a little guilty—3 or 4 days really isn't what I expected.

Then he added this request:

> Nate, do me another favor—If anything should happen to me—and there's a chance because lieutenants have been known to get hurt in wars—and if a question ever comes up about Barb ever getting married again—please exert your influence in favor of it. I hate to think of Barb being deprived of a home and children because of me. Perhaps you think I'm being over-dramatic, but I say this sincerely and with no more desire for histrionics than one does in making out a will, taking out insurance, etc.

The request said a lot about my uncle and his relationships with both Barbara and Nathan. I have no idea whether Nathan eventually felt he needed to pass this message on to Barbara.

After leaving, I suspect that Phil wrote to Barbara frequently. He certainly referred to her frequently in his journal and, in fact, decided on the second day to change the form of the journal itself:

> This diary form is no good. I constantly think in terms of "you"—the "you" being Barb. So I'll drop the impersonal construction and make this a letter—to be delivered after the war.

Many of his journal references to Barbara were professions of love that reflect the ardor of a panting teenager. For example:

God! I love you darling. When you've seen what I've seen.
. . . everything that is good, elevating and inspiring can
be found only in our love. In this world people look for
something to cling to and I have found what I need—that is
you and your love.

We will have such wonderful times when we are together
again. Why can't I tell these people how simple it is to have a
naïve faith in and love for you. Why can't I describe to them
the ultimate in satisfaction which comes from the knowledge
that you love me. All day I have gone about this ship—
bursting with love for you—wanting to tell everyone—
wanting to keep it a secret between you and me. Wanting to
be with you. Wanting you.

Yes I'm mad—completely and totally mad with love of you. . . .
I want to start our life together.

In another entry, Phil tells Barbara that he regrets not being in danger much—"though I have never once asked to avoid hazardous duty"—and hopes to get a front line assignment once they land:

. . . so perhaps I am fortunate—and perhaps I have been
saved for other things by the Fates. . . . I have been saved
for you, my dearest—and to me you mean life's end—final
goal—you mean life itself.

He also spoke about Barbara to everyone he met aboard the *Dunera* and elsewhere as well, usually showing them her picture. At a point my research led me to Jack Del Monte of Long Island, New York. Jack was in Phil's tank platoon for about a month. He was a wonderful person (he died, unfortunately, just before this book was published) and he and I became friends. He had a razor-sharp and detailed memory of his war experiences and many other things. But when I first called Jack out of the blue, I doubted he'd recall my uncle sixty-six years after knowing him. Instead, Jack's first words to me were, "Sure I remember Phil—and wasn't his wife's name Barbara?"

Jack Del Monte with the author in 2014

Jack Del Monte in the army

War

6

Aboard the *Dunera*

A French aspirant named Galula

By the time Phil landed in North Africa in October 1943, the Allies had won the war there and invaded Italy. Although the Italians surrendered immediately, the Germans controlled the nation and deployed large numbers of troops to defend against the invasion. Before Phil got to Italy, the Allies had climbed up the boot past Naples, taken by the British on October 7, and had advanced to what was known as the *Winter* or *Gustav Line*, north of Naples and about seventy-five miles south of Rome, the next major objective of the Allies. In the spring, the allies continued their advance toward Rome and captured it on June 4, 1944.

I had difficulty tracking Phil's location during his first ten months in Africa and Europe. One complication was that he was "assigned," that is he was given temporary assignments rather than being specifically attached to a military unit, so unit records were of no help to me. Another complication was that Phil's personnel records along with those of most World War II veterans were destroyed in a major fire at the St. Louis Military Records Center in 1973. However, from several brief comments in letters and the journal, I learned that he served primarily as a translator in Special Services. One letter gives a bit more detail:

> In Translation, I handled all sorts of secret documents,
> battle orders, requisitions, plans, maps, training documents,
> and I shook with excitement as I turned out translations of
> intelligence materials obtained from the French underground

dealing with location of enemy pill boxes, the mining of bridges, disposition of enemy troops, etc.

After nine months in this position, Phil became very frustrated. In a letter to Nathan on July 6, 1944, he unloaded his feelings, giving full vent to his frustration:

> By the way, Nate, I have a subject which I'd like to discuss, and although this letter was not meant to be a "gripe" letter this is a subject which has concerned me and no doubt you have heard something of it before.
>
> Let me preface my remarks by saying that I'm loyal to my country and I fully feel the responsibility of a commissioned officer—more so, I feel, than many of my equals and superiors. I am willing to do my job whatever that might be and do it with the greatest possible exertion on my part. I think that I have done so and am doing so.
>
> But I have had great ideas on what I would do in my army career. I was looking forward to my commission in 1939 when most of my fellows were having Peace Rallies. . . . I did well in my R.O.T.C. career and as Honor Graduate I was given a chance to apply for a Regular Army commission which I did, and which fell through. . . .
>
> I did well at O. C. S., at Battle Training, and in the 10th Armored Division, receiving two "Excellent" ratings. I was ready for my 1st in that organization when I was shipped overseas. . . .
>
> In Africa I applied for Special Services—gun-running to Southern France or even Yugoslavia. I trekked from place to place seeking a job. I saw 30 non-French speaking officers get assigned with the French. I begged to be sent to the Front in any capacity.
>
> I end up in Italy and after a couple of months I'm attached which means that I'm not on a T/O [Table of Organization] and so no matter how much I do or how hard I try I cannot receive a promotion.
>
> The situation has become worse and worse. It has been a long time since I've seen a tank or even handled a platoon. . . .

At present I may get an assignment. I'm working hard to organize a new set-up, but I've been told that they may not be able to use me. . . .

But here is how I feel at present. I have a priority from Lt. Gen. Devers on French speaking assignments and I've done all the other things in my power to find a place. After nine months overseas I have become convinced that I am not needed. I cite as proof the fact that I have never once been given a job where I might prove my worth or get a promotion. . . . If this present thing falls through, I am going to request to be put on the Reserve inactive list, or that my resignation be accepted. Perhaps I could be drafted as a private, but at least they seem to have uses for privates and that's more than they've found for me in all this time overseas.

A month later, Phil got his new assignment. He would take part in Operation Dragoon—a major Allied invasion of southern France mirroring the Normandy invasion two months earlier in northern France. He headed to Naples to board the HMT *Dunera*, an officers' boat in Dragoon's armada, and his enthusiasm returned. He was on his way to help liberate France—taking part in "a rather historic moment, and I'm somewhere in the middle of it." He was happy to be out of his prior work, and excited to be part of the operation that he felt would "be the straw that breaks the Nazis' back."

On August 9, 1944, when he stepped aboard the British transport ship *Dunera*, Phil folded several 8½" x 11" sheets of brownish, onionskin paper in half and began his journal: "During these past months I have often thought of keeping a diary or journal. . . ." He dated his entries, numbered pages as he went, and wrote in small handwriting on both the front and back of sheets to conserve paper. Almost the entire ninety-six-page journal was written during his seven days aboard ship and first three days ashore.

It is odd that this journal, written on a ship advancing toward battle, would provide my most vivid portrayal of Phil's character. But the trip offered several days when Phil had few assignments; and the specter of the invasion provided a special reason to both socialize

The *Dunera*, 1937

and reflect on life. By August 14, as final briefings and landing preparations began, Phil's attention began to shift, and soon after, entries became brief and sporadic before stopping altogether.

The *Dunera* was an officers' ship, transporting both high-ranking officers and lowly ones like Second Lieutenant Levy. Its officers included 950 Americans, 33 Frenchmen, and a smattering of Englishmen. Apparently this special cargo merited a reasonably plush transport vessel, for the *Dunera* had a music room. Phil headed to this room immediately upon boarding.

> A French officer is playing the piano and he plays rather
> well. He is commercial rather than artistic. One gets the
> impression that he puts too much "feeling" into this playing.
> He plays all the regular stock of Rimsky-Korsikov [*sic*],
> Liszt, Mozart, et al—all light works.

Then Phil expressed the hope that he will take up the piano again and explains why his "children will be exposed to music"— "its elevating effects on the mind" . . . "a sense of independence" . . . "personal satisfaction from accomplishment." This entry offers a powerful impression of Phil's musical proficiency and the role of music in his life.

Phil spent much time during the voyage socializing, but he also enjoyed being alone. He read, studied language, wrote letters, and wrote in his journal, reporting on significant daily events aboard ship and often reflecting on them:

> We are served by dark-skinned Indians who retain their picturesque turbans and gowns. They are extremely nice— always trying to serve you. . . . I can't help but think . . . as we go out on this mission of liberation that India is kept in subjugation. It's a problem which I am willing to ignore momentarily in order not to criticize our allies, but Freedom is not a thing to be ignored. The U.S. should be able to put its weight on the side of India after the war and thus force England to free her. . . .

This entry was marked "delete" by a censor, and is one of many sentences and paragraphs in the journal marked with that term or with red marks. For some reason, those portions were merely flagged but not blacked out.

I expected military censors to watch for material that, if mailed and intercepted or otherwise seized, might reveal valuable strategic information to the enemy. But apparently censors also watched for material that could offend allies or convey unfavorable views of America to enemies or allies, for all the censor's journal markings involved comments of this type. Phil wrote angrily about "those two French ambulance drivers who called Americans cowards." . . . " [**Delete**]. Phil told of his own difficulties getting a pistol on the *Dunera*, adding that the French seem to get supplies on board quite easily. [**Delete**]. Phil wrote of a French officer who "thought that it was very intelligent of our Army to provide its men with women through the ANC and the WACS. . . ." [**Delete.**]

When I introduced Barbara earlier, I mentioned Phil's expressions of love for her and quoted several such expressions from the journal. On the second day aboard the *Dunera*, Phil showed Barbara's picture to a Frenchman who "fell in love" with her. This led Phil to think extensively about her and to decide to change the journal into a long letter to her—"to be delivered after the war." Phil noted that this Frenchman said how every day puts him further away from the sweet days he left, but Phil—now addressing his remarks in the journal to Barbara—prefers to say, "every day puts me one closer to the sweeter days . . . which are to come. . . . When I think of the wonderful things we can have together, I shake with anticipation."

Another theme that arises regularly in the journal is Phil's pride in America. For example, he recalled this incident from Italy that made him "proud to be an American and proud to be an officer":

> . . . Lt. Crock and Sgt. Lutz were riding to town in our 3 ton truck. They approached a bridge and [stopped]. There ahead of them, was a cart. . . . The wheels had become lodged between the edge of the bridge and some planking. . . . The poor little animal pulling the cart tugged for dear life urged on by the cries of the old "paisan" who was pulling too. The animal was weak and emaciated and his feet couldn't find a firm footing on the smooth boards.
>
> [Crock and Lutz dismounted] and approached the cart. The paisan trembled for he knew he was in for it—having blocked an Army vehicle and made the officer stop.
>
> But his mouth dropped in astonishment as he saw the Lt. and the Sgt. each shoulder a wheel, lift the cart and start it rolling across the bridge. He saluted and was so delighted that he couldn't say anything—just half bow, salute, and mutter "grazie, tante grazie."

In another entry, he praised the army for its efficiency and America for its selfless sacrifice:

> I become sick and weak inside when I think of my beloved America squeezed dry of her resources in order to make thousands of ships, planes, guns, tanks, uniforms (of cloth which should have made cute little dresses for pretty little girls). I become ill when I think of the men killed and maimed . . . —a fight that we didn't want. We

have no imperialistic designs. We ask to be left alone
and now we have inflation, the threat of unemployment,
child delinquency, broken homes, debt, a nation rapidly
exhausting her supply of precious resources.

Then I am proud that we have been able to do what we
have done. That we have offered a hand to the suffering of
the world. That we can become mighty and yet retain the
qualities which make us a refreshing nation amongst the
polluted nations of the old world. . . .

The censors had no problem with these thoughts.

Occasionally Phil's pride is tempered with concern. In one
lengthy entry, he compliments America's massive, well-planned,
well-implemented invasions of Europe but wonders whether we can
"apply as much force, energy, foresight, to winning the Peace."

It is easy to call upon people to kill the Jap or the German.
People will sacrifice to fight [them], but will they fight
ignorance and poverty with equal energy.

We can publish propaganda denouncing the Jap . . . but
human ignorance and poverty which cause even more
suffering than the Jap . . . do not lend themselves to being the
object of "war" efforts. . . .

Phil envisions the post-war moment as a tremendous opportunity
for declaring a different kind of war on ignorance and poverty in
"the greatest undertaking ever contemplated by the human mind."
But he wonders if we will "locate the driving and grinding force
for [this]." This entry touched me deeply, for twenty years almost
to the day after Phil wrote this entry, America's "War on Poverty"
was launched. Ultimately this "war" would have neither sufficient
resources nor sufficient staying power to be won, but it did capture
the allegiance of many young people, aiming them at the type of hope
Phil expressed. I was one of those young people, and the commitment
to fighting poverty remained as the central theme of my life work as a
poverty lawyer, a social worker, and a social welfare teacher.

Not all of Phil's time aboard the *Dunera* was leisure. He had several duties, and describes the most significant of them this way:

> I was given a job today. They made me Chief of Water Boiling
> and Distributing Facilities A. S. [Aboard Ship]. I was given
> an assistant and a three man detail (all French). We devised
> the system and put it into operation to provide hot water—
> plain and soapy for dish-washing activities on shipboard. The
> magnitude of the job and its importance overwhelm me. I
> imagine that I'll be put in for a Legion of Merit. I promoted
> my assistant to Sub-Chief and got him an assistant, thus giving
> us three men to supervise the three man detail.

Phil's humor and self-deprecation are particularly notable because he so badly wanted significant assignments and credit for doing them well. And it is quite to his credit that he took the work seriously. The job involved working in what was known as "the inferno," so Phil instituted a job rotation to make it more tolerable. He also altered the composition of his all-French work crew because of the unfairness of putting all of this work on Frenchmen when, as he noted, Americans on board outnumbered Frenchmen 950 to 33. Phil approaches this small, short-term task avidly and with fairness and humanity, signaling that he might have become a very fine manager.

The wry humor in Phil's description of being Chief of Water Boiling pops up elsewhere in the journal. "This ship is an extraordinary place," he writes. "It seems that there is always lots of pounding and scraping going on—and all of it around my cabin at the exact hour when I try to sleep." Another entry stretches humor a bit further:

> I attach hereto a piece of paper [it no longer was with the
> journal] and though discretion and good taste demand that it
> not be named I shall announce the fact that it is toilet paper
> for fear that that fact might not be recognized now that the
> paper had been torn from its "milieu." I have no proof that
> that is what it is—other than the fact that I found it in a box
> along the right side of a toilet seat.
> If this is what the English use and have used as "papier

hygienique" then it is not farfetched to see in it the root of all British imperialism. It doesn't come in rolls but is issued in envelopes like our sandpaper at home. And they have the audacity to label it "American Toilet Paper."

At several points Phil speaks of himself as gullible or naïve. For example, a French officer named Offstetter wonders if American "women are easy" and talks about how easy German and eastern French women are. Later in the journal Phil thinks of the many times overseas when he has had to wait as "friends" had their women in parks, on roof tops, in trucks. . . . "The world is funny," he concludes, "And most of the people whom I know—my circle—or former circle—are so damn naïve."

At another point, however, Phil seems oblivious to his own naïveté. He reports on telling a table of British officers a story that he felt was hilarious. He referred to "the well-known story" of Ben Franklin and Edward Gibbon, the English author of *The Rise and Fall of the Roman Empire*. Since I was unfamiliar with the story, I looked it up. There are several versions of it, but the gist is that Franklin visited England and wanted to meet Gibbon who refused. The rejection didn't diminish Franklin's admiration of the historian for he promptly promised to help Gibbon when he came to write the history of the decline and fall of the British Empire. Phil was stunned when none of the officers so much as smiled.

Phil enjoyed his time alone on the *Dunera*, but he particularly seemed to enjoy talking with shipmates. Most of his conversations were with French officers, usually Offstetter, Maxwell, Falco, Galula, or a combination of these men. This reflects Phil's great interest in his college major, the French language and culture. Conversations were wide ranging. They covered such topics as anticipated postwar problems, races and their prejudices, traits of cultures, love, rape, American women and French women, education in America, literature, De Gaulle, and so forth. Sometimes Phil was more listener than talker. For example, Phil mostly listened when Offstetter predicted challenges that France would face after the war: problems of integrating two million POWs back into society, or the possibility that the French would turn Hitler into a hero as they had done with Napoleon. However, in most conversations, Phil was a very active participant.

Some exchanges got a bit heated:

> I just had a loud argument with Galula on the subject of our invasion currency. I maintained that the French were "obliged" to take it. He said no. He told me that the people of Normandy just yesterday showed their confidence in us (by voting to accept American dollars). I said that it was very nice of the French people to express their confidence in us, in our cause, and in our victory, after 2-1/2 months of fighting, at least 80,000 American casualties—at least 12,000 killed....

Some other exchanges dealt with uncomfortable topics. For example, at one point Falco says that the French think of Corsicans as being "worse than a bunch of ... Jews." Phil immediately responds to this phrase and they have a healthy discussion. Reflecting on this incident later, Phil wrote:

> You know, he meant no harm and was just using a figure of speech like "Jewing someone down." I have decided that I cannot hold such statements against people anymore than I would want a Scotchman to feel offended when I say that someone is Scotch.

Phil's acceptance of these slurs as "figures of speech" surprised me. Of course, this was twenty years before Americans, with the social movements of the 1960s and beyond, began to scrutinize such ethnic stereotypes intensely. But his amiable response also might have been because he had experienced much more direct and abusive antisemitism. This was the case with many Jewish soldiers. Memoirs in *GI Jews* refer to insults like "Jew boy," "Kike," or a greeting of "*Heil Hitler*" routinely used by fellow soldiers. Some GIs faced prejudice from their superiors. The book's author concluded that, "In the European Theater, Jewish soldiers battled several foes. They fought the enemy, their fellow soldiers' prejudices, and their own anger at such hateful bias."[21]

Each Jewish soldier had to decide whether to ignore the slurs or address them. By and large, camaraderie trumped anger. A Jewish officer named Sugarman, for example, faced yet another antisemitic incident with his men. He was outraged and eventually confronted the soldier, but said in a letter home: "I remember how inadequate I felt when I tried to tell you how wonderful those guys on the beaches were last June [at the Normandy landing]. I wouldn't take back a word of it . . . but coupled with it comes a feeling of wonder. Wonder as to how such marvelous fighters can be such rotten people."[22]

Phil reported other slurs that bothered him more than the one by Falco. For example, when two female French ambulance drivers called Americans "cowards," Phil spent two journal pages imagining six retorts he might have made, but in the end, simply should have told them, "that they were beautiful but dumb, had they been beautiful." And late in his journal, Phil refers to a French officer making some derogatory remark about "the Jews and Arabs in Africa." Phil could "hardly restrain [himself] from punching him in the nose. I'm risking my neck for his country. . . ."

Phil enjoyed talking with many fellow officers, but right from the start, one seemed to fascinate him more than others:

> The interesting news of today is that I spent much of the afternoon and evening, and all the meal times with a French "aspirant" [a French officer-in-training] named Galula. He comes from Marseilles . . . businessman—large scale— international—soap and oils. Learned to speak English in France and speaks it well.

Galula and Phil had a lot in common. Both were young—Galula was twenty-six and Phil twenty-three—bright, articulate, and bilingual in French and English. Both had a deep knowledge of French culture. Both were low-ranked officers but had been through special officers' training. Both were also Jewish, although Galula never admitted this to Phil, saying only at a point in one of their long conversations, "I once dated a Jewish girl."

I mentioned earlier that a Frenchman had seen Barbara's picture and become smitten by her. That Frenchman was Galula:

> Our conversation started with his mentioning marriage and my vocal expression of my constant thought "I wish I were with my wife."
>
> I showed him your picture and he was struck with your beauty, but remarked even more on the intellectual force you possess. . . .
>
> He really raved over you and was sorrowed by the fact that we had such a short stay together. . . .

Then the conversation turned to women in general and Phil reports their repartee in some detail. Galula suggests that it must be difficult to remain true. Phil responds, "Yes and no. Being a fairly normal man I have sexual cravings, but it isn't hard to be true to [Barbara]." Galula pushes the inquiry, "But don't you love women?" Phil responds, "Yes I love them all . . . and tell my wife what I do with them [talk to them and maybe even dance with them]." "No, but you soon sleep with them," Galula counters. "Not I," says Phil. The light banter continues with Phil claiming full faithfulness to Barbara, and Galula wholly unable to fathom this possibility. Soon Galula is recounting his own personal exploits, which Phil records:

> In France one cannot be faithful. Why not? The women are so lovely and charming and they love one in such a fresh, good way that you simply can't resist them.
>
> Galula has been in love with a beautiful, intelligent Algerian girl for the past year. She is a widow with a child. He doesn't like widows, preferring divorcees, but he thinks divorce is bad if children are involved. Mostly he loves married women with children. He had two such women at once in France and prides himself on having prevented two divorces by loving these women. He was ready to marry another girl and "made a date for the beach . . . so he could see her legs—that was the only thing which he wasn't sure of

and he just couldn't marry her if her legs were no good." But he broke this date to go to Athens where he fell in love with another married woman with children. . . .

Then Galula returns to testing Phil's fidelity. He says how much he admires Phil—whom he "supposes" has found his true love. Phil counters that he doesn't merely "*suppose* it, he *knows* it." And then Galula shares a story. He says that he recently met an American lieutenant who had been married eight days before coming overseas and who now says he no longer loves his wife. . . . Phil denies that he has any such misgivings and, that night, as he describes this conversation in his journal, he reassures Barbara, "God! I love you darling. . . ."

A couple of days later, Phil is having dinner with Galula and a third person named Maxwell:

> Maxwell had heard from Galula that I had the most beautiful wife in the world who was clever and intelligent. . . . Galula continued to rave on about how he usually only likes lighter girls, but that henceforth he would prefer very dark haired girls—only as lovely as my wife.

I wanted to know whether Galula married a blond or a brunette, and I would later find out.

The dinner conversation shifts to the topic of "rape" and Phil reported on Galula's comments:

> Galula may have been kidding, but he seemed shocked to learn that rape (le viol) was a crime in the American Army. In rear areas he said it was criminal but not in battle areas and particularly not when it involved enemy women. . . . He mentioned that the Germans did it and that without rape and loot war was not worthwhile. I think because of that statement that he was pulling my leg. I'm very gullible you know. I explained that the sentence was death for rape. . . .

A later conversation with Galula convinced Phil that Galula

might not have been kidding about his views of rape. By the fifth day on board, Galula's constant sex-focused repartee seemed to be getting a bit tedious for Phil:

> Galula continues to bother me about you. You know—it's terribly difficult. It's bad enough just missing you, but with him here it's like missing you doubly.

Galula is the most memorable character in Phil's journal. He is compelling and occasionally annoying, often a charmer and a wonderful storyteller as well, apparently, as a womanizer and a tease. But, after everyone is supplied with a map of the landing area in southern France, it is Galula who helps Phil study the terrain of that area. Perhaps it is no surprise given that he was quite familiar with the French Riviera.

For five days Phil enjoyed some carefree moments in the midst of war. It was reminiscent, I imagine, of reflections and conversations he had back at college and with Nathan and with some boyhood friends. But as Dragoon's D-Day neared and activity aboard the *Dunera* turned back to war, this brief reminder of life as Phil once knew it was about to end—and not long after, life itself.

7

An Irony of Phil on the *Dunera*

A deplorable and regrettable mistake

Early on, I told you that my search for Phil led, at times, to off-the-highway adventures. Here's one of them.

Phil was not the first Jewish boy to board the *Dunera* when he boarded on August 9, 1944. Another, for example, was Walter Jonathan Foster, born Walter Fast in Vienna in 1923 to a wealthy entrepreneurial family. Walter was one of the ten thousand Jewish youngsters rescued by the Kindertransport during the year after Kristallnacht, and he ended up in England in 1939. Many of his relatives would die at the hands of the Nazis, so Walter was lucky and so was his father, a factory owner who was released from the Dachau concentration camp after signing over his factories. Walter later became an interpreter with the occupation forces in Germany after the war.[23]

Yet another Jewish boy to board the *Dunera* before Phil was Willy Field. Born Willy Hirschfeld in Bonn in 1920, Willy had been arrested by the Nazis the day after Kristallnacht and sent to Dachau, but he was able to escape to England after his employer arranged his release from the camp. Later Willy joined the Royal Armoured Corps, became a tank driver, took part in D-Day and survived five tanks. In Holland in September 1944, his tank suffered a direct hit and he was the sole survivor.[24]

Phil would have loved to talk with Walter and Willy. His journal showed how much he enjoyed conversations on the *Dunera* and he, of course, had a very special interest in Nazi antisemitism. But Walter and Willy boarded the *Dunera* at another time—July 10, 1940, at another place—Liverpool, England, and for another destination—the internment camps in Hay, New South Wales, Australia. They were two of about 2,000 Jewish refugees (all male) on board along with 200 Italian and 251 German prisoners of war and several dozen Nazi sympathizers. All were considered "enemy aliens" and were being shipped to incarceration in Australia. Collectively, the Jewish "boys" came to be known as "The Dunera Boys."

The Boys' story has been told by many.[25] Their voyage took fifty-seven days. The first day out, the boat was torpedoed but suffered only minor damage. The ship was badly overcrowded and supplies and facilities wholly inadequate—each twenty men had a piece of soap, clothing had been stored so they had no changes of attire, and they were given small food rations. Passengers were badly mistreated by the British guards and there were daily beatings. Dysentery ran through the ship, possessions such as wedding rings and watches were confiscated by the guards, and items like medicine and false teeth tossed overboard. One passenger likened the voyage to that of a slave ship. The medical examiner who boarded the ship immediately after it landed was appalled at conditions and made a report that led to a court martial of the officer-in-charge.

When the *Dunera* docked in Sydney on September 6, 1940, many Australians were not eager to accept this boatload of Jews. The country had a longstanding, very well-assimilated Jewish community, but it also had a history of opposition to further Jewish immigration. In 1928, for example, Australian Prime Minister Stanley Bruce said that he wanted Australians to remain "essentially a British and white people" (generally Jews were not considered "white" at that time), and this was a view held by all major political parties at the time.[26] There even was opposition to the newcomers expressed by many in Australia's Jewish community where, over time, assimilation permitted them to be treated as British and therefore "white." They didn't want to undermine their status in Australia so, as one writer stated, "Australian Jews shared the general xenophobia of Australians."[27]

The initial roundup of "enemy aliens" in England was carried out under an order of May 12, 1940, from Winston Churchill. Only two days earlier Churchill had become prime minister, replacing Neville Chamberlain, and it was a particularly precarious moment. During the next six weeks, Germany invaded and conquered Belgium, Holland, and France, and only the Miracle at Dunkirk (May 26 to June 3) saved over 300,000 British, French, and Belgian troops from slaughter or surrender after they were cut off by the Germans. Churchill would give his "finest hour" speech on June 18, but on June 4 he gave a speech entitled, "Wars Are Not Won By Evacuation" (reflecting on Dunkirk) and he briefly explained his "enemy alien" order:

> I know there are a great many people affected by the orders ... who are the passionate enemies of Nazi Germany. I am very sorry for them, but we cannot, at the present time and under the present stress, draw all the distinctions which we should like to do.[28]

In 1941, after complaints by Jewish inmates, a report by the Quaker Friends Society, and the bombing of Pearl Harbor, the prisoners were reclassified as "friendly aliens" and released. They were offered Australian residency and about one thousand accepted while most others returned to England. Most enlisted in the Australian or English armies. Eventually, following an official inquiry, each was compensated with a grant of 35,000 British pounds. Later, when Churchill reversed his "enemy aliens" order, he called it "a deplorable and regrettable mistake."

The aliens order had been very atypical of Churchill, a consistent and outspoken supporter of Jews, but not atypical in the world of our allies at the time. The Evian Conference in 1938, mentioned earlier, was a prominent illustration of this. Despite extensive rhetoric from representatives of all thirty-two nations at the conference, only the Dominican Republic offered even a modicum of help. The delegate from Australia, Colonel Tom White, was particularly clear as to why.

HMT DUNERA AT PYRMONT
SEPT. 6 1940

| The *Dunera* in Sydney, Australia, September 6, 1940 | Dunera Boys embarking in Sydney, September 6, 1940 |

"Under the circumstances Australia cannot do more. . . . It will no doubt be appreciated also that, as we have no real racial problem, we are not desirous of importing one."[29]

Another infamous example of indifference involved the so-called "voyage of the damned." Just prior to the outbreak of war in 1939, the German ocean liner, *St. Louis,* brought nearly one thousand German Jewish refugees to Cuba where they were denied asylum. Asylum was in turn denied by South and Central American nations, by the United States, and finally by Canada. The ship sailed back to deposit its cargo in Germany, but at the last minute England, Belgium, France, and the Netherlands each took in several hundred passengers. Tragically, the Nazis conquered all of these nations except England shortly thereafter, and many of the refugees were sent to Nazi camps where few survived.

But the reasonably rapid reversal by England and Australia of Churchill's decision also illustrated that Eugenics-reinforced antisemitism was fading. It would change quite dramatically after the

Reunion of Dunera Boys, 1990

war in the wake of unimaginable lessons from liberated Nazi camps and the Nuremberg Trials, with the proliferation of ecumenical programs such as those promoted by the National Conference of Christians and Jews (NCCJ). Nathan and Norma got heavily involved in NCCJ in South Bend, and quite likely Phil and Barbara would have as well.

I knew something of pre-war attitudes and post-war changes, but I knew nothing of one extensive effort in coexistence during the war. The US Armed Forces insisted that its chaplains adopt and practice a new concept, the notion that America has a Judeo-Christian heritage. Prior to the war Protestants didn't consider Catholics to be Christians, and neither religion acknowledged Jews as vital to their respective heritages. But the new concept envisioned Jews, Catholics, and Protestants as equals, united by a common set of beliefs and traditions including democracy and freedom that were distinctly American. The military policy expected chaplains to preach Judeo-Christian values, offer ecumenical worship, and minister to soldiers of all religions. It also tried to provide special worship services for soldiers to observe the holy days of their faith, and urged soldiers of other faiths to fill in for those attending these services. The policy wasn't always successful, but it was widely practiced and sometimes had astounding impact as is evident in this story of the liberation of Aachen, France, in 1944, reported by a Jewish GI.[30]

Yom Kippur, the most holy day observed by Jews, occurred in September 1944, but services that year could not be offered to Jewish soldiers of the First Infantry Division (known as "the Big Red One") until there was a lull in the fighting. The first lull occurred in early October with the surrender of German forces at Aachen. The Germans had suffered extraordinary losses, and General Huebner, commander of the American troops, allowed the German commander, Colonel Wilck, to address his defeated troops soon after the surrender. The POWs were gathered in the square outside the famous Aachen Cathedral surrounded by about five hundred Americans. Wilck reminded his troops that they were still German and urged them to silently give a "*Heil Hitler*" noting that Huebner had prohibited an actual salute.

> Then Huebner took the microphone and reassured "every man of Jewish faith in our outfit that . . . they'd have the chance to participate in a makeshift service for Yom Kippur . . . inside the Aachen Cathedral. . . . Every man of Jewish faith who wants to take part will immediately proceed" into the cathedral.

The defeated Nazis watched. "They were waiting to see how many Jews were wearing the Big Red One. [A Sergeant] who was about as Jewish as a pork chop, turned" and headed into "the cathedral, as if to say 'stick that up your *Mein Kampf!*' Every other dogface in the square followed" him too. "On that occasion, everybody was Jewish."

Perhaps Phil, alive at the time and stationed just 150 miles from Aachen, heard about this moving moment.

8

Did Galula Make It Through?

None was as important

Here's another off-the-highway adventure. This one is about Galula, the quirky and charismatic French officer that Phil met on the *Dunera*. The name seemed unusual, so I decided to Google it. Up popped "David Galula" and he was clearly the officer from the *Dunera*. One citation was to a 2010 article by Ann Marlowe. It is largely biographical and reveals that Galula had indeed survived the war. He had gone on to be a career officer in the French Army, but died in 1967 of cancer at the age of forty-eight. Why, I wondered, was he the subject of a 2010 article if he had died forty years earlier?

Marlowe tells us that David Galula was born in 1919:

> . . . to a prosperous Jewish merchant clan of Sfax, Tunisia. He was the sixth of seven children, and the only boy. David's great-grandfather had been a rich merchant . . . [and] his grandfather was an olive oil producer and . . . dean of the Jewish community in Sfax.
>
> . . . The family believed that they were descended not from European immigrants but from indigenous Jews. There is a town called Galula near the Libyan border of Tunisia, and the Galula family says that residents converted to Judaism about two thousand years ago.
>
> . . . The Galulas were secular and worldly, and there were intellectuals and scientists in the family as well as businesspeople.[31]

Galula never divulged to Phil that he was Jewish, and Phil never suspected it. Apparently this was a pattern in Galula's life, as I learned from a fine biography of Galula that was published soon after Marlowe's article. Its author, Alain Cohen, reported a conversation with Ruth, David's wife, in which she said that David was proud of his Jewish heritage but rarely self-identified as Jewish and could readily conceal that fact:

> . . . socially he wasn't hampered . . . as he might have been in those years . . . by his belonging to the Jewish faith. He did not look Jewish, and his last name did not give it off either. David never reacted when he heard disparaging comments being made about Jews by fellow officers. There were lots of these comments thrown about. I knew that he was proud inside of who he was."[32]

Marlowe also notes David's magnetism, something that Phil recognized immediately upon meeting him aboard the *Dunera*. She says that David's father was reputed to be "charming, brilliant and a great raconteur," and adds that this is "a description many have applied to David as well." She identifies some exploits in David's non-military life that reflected this charisma. He was a daring adventurer, an accomplished horseman, and an excellent golfer. He met and impressed many famous people and at times lived the high life. Using the pen name Jean Caran, he wrote a novel, *The Tiger's Whisker*.[33] He also became the model for a character, Jean Leone, in Seymour Topping's novel, *The Peking Letter*.[34] Topping had met Galula years earlier in China and described him, Marlowe reports, as a "fun-loving guy" with a "lust for life." Marlowe tells us that Leone, in the novel, "is depicted as a worldly cynic who frequented the 'joy girls' of the city's brothels." Marlow concludes, "Galula is universally recalled as charming, pleasant to be around, brilliant, and energetic. . . . He was also physically daring and intellectually curious."

Of course nothing I have mentioned so far explains why a Frenchman who died over forty years ago would suddenly be a popular subject in America. The answer involves two events, Galula's military career and the United States' war in Iraq.

As with Phil, it was surprising that Galula became a soldier. His family had no military tradition "nor did martial spirit run deep in the Sephardic community [Jews from Spain and Portugal] of that era."[35] Apparently his military interest was sparked by an uncle in the French Army. Although David had been an indifferent student, he suddenly set his sights on attending St. Cyr, the West Point of France, studied hard, and passed the admissions exam. He graduated in 1939, and left France for North Africa shortly after Germany conquered France and expelled Jewish officers from the French Army. (His uncle was Catholic so he was not expelled from the army, but he opted to join de Gaulle's Free French Army, served in North Africa, was captured by the Germans, and died in the Dachau concentration camp.)

In Africa, Galula had various assignments, including being a spy in Tangiers. It is not altogether clear who he was working for in that capacity, but Cohen believes it was the Allies, either the British or the Americans. When the Allies secured North Africa in 1943, Galula joined the French Committee on National Liberation (an amalgam of two competing French liberation forces headed by General de Gaulle and General Giraud). Eventually, he and his unit joined the forces of Operation Dragoon.

After landing on the beaches of the Riviera, Galula led a military intelligence platoon for the remainder of the war. Later, he became a military strategist and was sent to China. There he learned Chinese, was captured and then released by the Chinese Communists, and remained in China to study the guerilla tactics of Mao. At a diplomatic reception in China, he met Ruth Morgan, an American from California who was with the US State Department, part of the first group of women recruited by the Department to serve overseas. She was not Jewish, and in 1949, they were married in a church in France.

Galula became a strategist in the French war in Indo-China (Vietnam) and began at that point to develop strategies for addressing guerilla insurgency. In 1956, at the age of thirty-seven, Galula volunteered to return to combat in Algeria where France was trying

David Galula military ID card, 1945

to suppress Algerian rebels seeking independence. As commander in a small town there, he was able to try out some of his counterinsurgency (COIN) strategies.

In 1960, Galula came to the United States and studied for six months at the Armed Forces Staff College in Norfolk, Virginia. Soon after, he served on a panel of COIN experts called together by the RAND Corporation. In 1962, with the help of General William Westmoreland, who was superintendent of West Point at the time, Galula received an appointment to teach at the Harvard Center for International Affairs. There he became friends with the Center's associate director, Henry Kissinger. The Galulas' adopted son, Daniel, played with the Kissinger children. When David's hopes for a permanent appointment at Harvard fell through, he returned to France and wrote two books on COIN: *Counterinsurgency Warfare,*

David Galula in later life

and *Pacification in Algeria 1956–1958*.[36] At the time, these books were not widely read.

The Iraq war began with the "shock and awe" bombing of Baghdad by the United States in 2003, followed immediately by President George W. Bush's declaration of victory in his famous "Mission Accomplished" speech aboard the USS *Abraham Lincoln*. Then, of course, the real war began. It was a guerilla war rather than a traditional war, with large-scale air, land, and sea confrontations. Quickly our nation realized that the nature of warfare had changed. Wars now would entail countering guerilla insurgencies. The president appointed General David Petraeus to command our troops in Iraq, and shortly afterward asked him to head a task force to rewrite the army's manual on war. The task force completed its work in December 2006, releasing its new *Field Manual (FM) 3-24 (US*

Army Manual, 2006). This manual frequently cites Galula's work and thought, and in a foreword to the University of Chicago Press edition of the *Manual*, General Petraeus says: "Of the many books that were influential in the writing of [FM] 3-24, perhaps none was as important as David Galula's *Counterinsurgency Warfare: Theory and Practice.*"[37]

Suddenly many Americans were interested in David Galula.

The *Manual* adopts Galula's central principle of counterterrorism, that armies must become embedded in communities rather than isolated in well-defended enclaves. As they demand the allegiance of villagers, they also need to earn that allegiance by working with villagers on issues of highest local concern, such as schools, health, and children. An often-cited quotation from Galula appearing in the *Manual* (at page 2-42) caught my attention:

> To confine soldiers to purely military functions . . .
> would be senseless. The soldier must then be prepared to
> become a propagandist, a social worker, a civil engineer, a
> schoolteacher, a nurse, a boy scout. But only for as long as he
> cannot be replaced, for it is better to entrust civilian tasks to
> civilians.[38]

What caught my eye specifically was the notion of soldiers being "social workers." Some commentators refer to Galula's general approach to counterinsurgency as "armed social work." My sister and I are social workers, and Barbara and our mother Norma were also. To a social worker, Galula's approach simply adopts a core tenet of our profession: Start with the client; focus first on matters that the client considers vital.

In the small town where Galula experimented with his approach, he hired villagers to do such things as build and operate a dispensary and a school. Noting the local oppression of women, he created policies and opportunities that emancipated them, knowing that this would likely earn their allegiance to France. I'm sure the Galula approach would have interested Phil, for, as you may recall, he wondered how America and the world might fight poverty and ignorance after the war.

You also may recall the conversation aboard the *Dunera* in which Galula claimed to prefer light-haired women until Phil showed him Barbara's picture and Galula suddenly became infatuated with brunettes. Obviously he was teasing my earnest uncle, but I wanted to know the hair color of the woman he eventually married. I e-mailed Ann Marlowe and asked, but she didn't know. She had interviewed a gray-haired Ruth Galula. Upon learning that Ruth had returned to California, I tried to reach her and learned that she had died only a few months earlier. But I also learned that her son Daniel had been living with her and had moved away after she died. I was able to find and call him. He spoke with great pride about his father who had died when Daniel was quite young, and with great excitement he told me of the about-to-be-released biography by Alain Cohen.

I ended our conversation by telling Daniel the hair story and asked the color of his mother's hair. With a chuckle he said, "Brunette."

9

Into Combat

Message to Garcia and all that sort of stuff

"Another debarkation drill," Phil began his August 14 journal entry aboard the *Dunera*, an indication that he had shifted gears back to war after his five-day hiatus,

> ...and the efficiency and good order is a joy to behold. Split second timing. I'm a bit dizzy with all the history making events going on about me. Our army continues to distribute books, pamphlets, maps, equipment—it has foreseen every detail and I am genuinely proud of the army.

He adds to the list of distributions—"atabrine, salt, K Rations, D Ration, cigarettes . . . a Guide book to France, currency, Seventh Army patches. . . ."

Phil also received his new assignment: "aside from translating and liaison I have been briefed upon my courier duties."

> Once the beachhead is established the regular A. T. C. plane can be used to carry secret documents and valuable papers and messages from ____ to ____. In the meantime we must improvise means. We will travel by boat truck, P. T. boat, plane, parachute, or any other method necessary to carry out our mission. . . . We will then be used as couriers to the front line divisions and for various and sundry odd missions. It looks like we'll have an exciting time of it.

The *Dunera* passed between Corsica and Sardinia, nearing

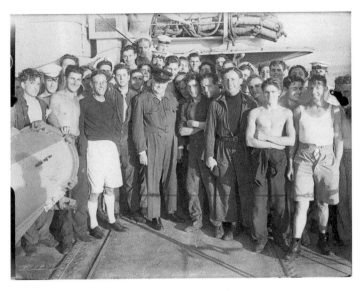

Churchill aboard the HMS *Kimberly*, about August 15, 1944

its destination, the French Riviera. Around it a vast armada had gathered. Phil saw the command ship (the *Catoctin*) carrying General Alexander Patch, commander of the Sixth Army Group as well as Vice Admiral H. Kent Hewitt, commander of naval operations for Dragoon, and General Jean de Lattre de Tassigny, commander of the French troops. Phil also saw the *Lorraine* that his French friends must have pointed out. It was the oldest ship in the French fleet and, in 1939, had carried French gold to the United States for safekeeping before the Nazis invaded.

Probably Phil and his crew didn't realize that Winston Churchill was also nearby, aboard the H. M. S. *Kimberly*, to watch Dragoon's D-Day landing. He had opposed the operation, fearing that fighting on two fronts would dilute the allied effort in Europe, but Eisenhower insisted on this second invasion from the south, and his opinion prevailed. The mission was originally called "Operation Anvil" and that name is still used in various US Army publications. One story explains that "Dragoon" was the name demanded by Churchill as a subtle slur since he felt "dragooned"—forced—into accepting the operation.[39]

The full armada consisted of "approximately 885 ships and landing craft sailing under their own power. On the decks of this armada were loaded nearly 1,375 smaller landing craft. Exclusive of naval crews, the convoys carried roughly 151,000 troops and some 21,400 trucks, tanks, tank destroyers, prime-movers, bulldozers, tractors, and other vehicles." Soon Admiral Hewitt, commander of the naval phase of Dragoon, would give his report that "all convoys sailed as planned without incident and rendezvous was effected as scheduled," and naval historian, Samuel Eliot Morrison, described Dragoon as "an example of an almost perfect amphibious operation from the point of view of training, timing, Army-Navy-Air Force cooperation, performance, and results."[40]

Phil wrote, "Tomorrow—15 August 1944 is 'D' Day. 'H' hour is 0800 hours. We eat at 7:15. After that we can only wait and hope." He was well-briefed on the landing plan and described it in some detail:

> Tonight, at midnight, Commandos commence their operations on both of our flanks. At 0550 tomorrow a 2 hour, 10 minute aerial and naval barrage will commence. At 0800, 3 American divisions assault the beaches. These will be followed by French armored and infantry forces. British and American gliders and paratroop operations will be carried on to disorganize the enemies [sic] rear.

His account aligns with historical accounts of the assault. Three clusters of divisions landed on a total of eleven Riviera beaches. Phil was in "Delta," the center cluster with its three American divisions, each landing on separate, adjacent beaches. The Third Infantry Division landed to Phil's left, and it included Audie Murphy who would become the war's most decorated soldier and later a famous actor. On D-Day, Murphy earned the Distinguished Service Cross for heroic action performed shortly after seeing his best friend killed.

Phil didn't expect to sleep well on the eve of D-Day, but he did. He recalled dreaming that his grandfather asked if he had been *dovening* (praying) and also dreaming about seeing the girls at Alpha

Epsilon Phi, the University of Michigan sorority where Barbara had been president. He was up at 5:30 a.m. and the naval guns opened on schedule.

During the day, Phil read a book—*Citizen of Westminster,* by British silent screen star turned novelist, Joan Morgan. He wondered "what type of person she was" and simultaneously noted the irony that "a war is raging about me and I am reading literature." News came in on BBC radio that the assault was thought to be going well. When BBC reported that Patton was placed in command of the Third Army, the Normandy troops in the north, and that Congress had promoted him, everyone cheered. Apparently Patton was very popular with these officers.

As Phil watched events on shore, suddenly there was an alert as a German plane attacked. It met anti-aircraft fire from surrounding ships and eventually escaped without doing damage, but Phil felt vulnerable on deck and expressed his first worry that he could have been killed. Phil and his fellow officers didn't disembark that day.

The next day, after "a fine night's sleep," Phil finished his book and wrote in his journal, "Think we'll land today. I hope so." His next entry began on a new page and was a continuation of August 16:

> Well I got my wish. I'm on the shores of France. We were ordered to report to our mustering stations. I put on the heavy, poorly designed equipment our Army uses—(just a gripe—not quite the truth) and reported down to "E" Deck. . . .
>
> After the usual wait we . . . climbed over the side—down a ladder 2-1/2 stories high. A brief ride in the L. C. [landing craft] and then a short march on shore. M. P.'s direct traffic. . . . We marched up to the open side of a hill and here I sit sweating in the hot sun. The beach is nice white sand—sand which has seen the rich of the world—who spent their vacations here.

Phil sat in the sun about three yards from the tape that marked the area cleared of German mines.

2 yards away from me is a French commandant [major]. I said, a moment ago, "Eh bien, mon commandant, ça vous plaît d'être en France." You can well imagine it has been 4 years since he last saw France.

He registered his disgust at forest fires that raged nearby, apparently set by the Germans who cut down thousands of trees to clear their view for firing at the invaders. "All needless waste disgusts me," Phil reflected, "So War is the most disgusting thing of all." He ended the day's entries with "Here we sit—waiting for orders."

Writing in the journal a day later, Phil apologized for not completing the prior day's entry, but things had gotten hectic. His unit on the beach received orders and "plodded inland" carrying their heavy gear. Phil felt quite in shape ("I could have double-timed") and noted that "The French cheered us at every farm" and every town. When the group stopped to rest, Phil and the French Commandant he had spoken to earlier kept going and joined the group ahead of them. As they continued on, suddenly "we were stopped by two bullets cracking over our heads. Down in the ditch. A machine gun burst."

Surrounded by superiors, Phil waited for an order, but none was given. He wanted to act and sought permission from a "full colonel" to join two others and go toward the house where the shots were fired. Permission was granted. The three headed toward the house but bullets came from another house and then from another.

> It was very movie-like. So, for 2-1/2 hours I went sniper-hunting in the hills. I succeeded in getting shot at 8 more times, and never fired one shot myself.

They continued on and Phil describes special things that happened during the march and sniper hunts:

> I'll tell you about the modern house in which perfect English was spoken. Two fleeting figures in the garden, the peasant who directed me from a window to outflank the sniper, and the old man who fired a shot to warn me, and then proudly showed me the tiny rusty automatic and the twenty odd

rounds which [he had buried four years earlier and taken out when the Americans landed on D-Day].

Phil recalled an old woman who said "voi, voi" for "oui, oui," and, linguist that he was, he comments on differences in accents between this French and Parisian French. "As we marched along we noticed great numbers of Negro [sic] soldiers who had beaten us ashore." The French people sang gleefully, and "an old red-faced man with tears streaming down his face" came out to embrace the French troops. Everyone, Phil noted, was glad to see the soldiers but they were especially happy to see the Free French soldiers—and "the women were good looking and all of them had carefully done up hair." He went to Free French headquarters in town and learned that some of their number had just been killed storming a German pillbox. He saw the dead bodies there. Here and there during the day, he continued to hunt snipers.

Phil found a swanky hotel to stay in that first night ashore (August 16) but was displaced by higher-ranking officers, and eventually Phil and Lieutenants Hecht and Hernandez found a room in a residence. They paid the young daughter of the family and then went for a walk. They spoke to an old man "who gave us wine. I pumped water for an old lady." Then Phil returned to the residence while Hecht and Hernandez continued "to work on a little 'deal'" the latter had cooked up.

> Soon it was dark. . . . As I was about to approach the
> window which was serving as a door people poured out
> into the street to watch the flac over the port. It is quite a
> show. . . . I had left my helmet in the house filled with water
> with which I had planned to wash. I knew that it had been
> a mistake to leave it there when I heard the screaming of a
> bomb. God! I was scared. I couldn't make it to the window.
> I did not know of any shelter, and at that moment the young
> girl came running up the street. She tripped fell and sat there
> looking frightened and bleeding from her leg.
> All this happened together and it seemed an eternity that
> the bomb screamed through. I grabbed the girl, threw her

against the curb and threw myself on top of her. Then the bomb hit. I could feel myself tremble. Bricks, dust, rubble tumbled down. Women cried. The girl was frightened. She asked me if we'd be safe in the "cave." I said yes so she took me by the hand and led me down there. I helped lots of old women and men down the stairway. . . . I told them there was nothing to fear.

The old man who had given Phil wine earlier was there and had four wounds. Phil "fixed him up with [his] aid pack" and took him out to the aid station. "They had no time for him. So I picked my way through the mass of bodies to get bandages and sulpha. God! That was more horrible than the last mess I saw." Phil saw two dead children and mangled bodies and legs and blood everywhere—"The bastardly Germans had dropped anti-personnel fragmentation bombs on the city." He helped more people and eventually walked up to headquarters and slept on the floor. There he learned that Hecht and Hernandez were both injured in the raid.

"Not much happened," Phil reported on August 18, and then he mentioned some small things. The Frenchman, whom Phil "fixed up" the night before, invites him for a drink. "Another old codger" tells Phil of lies spread by the Germans that Americans had run out of gasoline and equipment, so the war would end soon. A paratrooper speaks very highly of the Free French resistance work—but also notes that resisters have brought out their guns now and "are half-crazy and go out to kill Germans throwing caution to the winds."

Since Phil's personnel records had been burned in the St. Louis fire, I had little idea where Phil was at this point, but the only notable event that Phil reported on August 18 helped me locate him.

> We had a German general here. Our general had him in for a chat and for some supper. He [the German general] was travelling by American jeep. . . . He had a steamer trunk gaily decorated with the stickers of places he had visited. But he won't get around much anymore.

Captured German General Bieringer being transported to
US Seventh Army Headquarters, August 18, 1944

While the prisoner went in for a "chat" with "our general" (General Patch), his orderly sat in the jeep.

> GIs were starting to congregate around the prisoner. There were some [officers] in the vicinity. I looked on for a moment, a GI was about to offer the prisoner a cigarette and another was [trying to communicate]. I stepped over and in a low voice said: "Don't you men know that it is against the policy of our government to permit fraternization with prisoners of war?" The crowd just melted away and some of the GIs looked at me . . . with their mouths hanging open.
>
> Besides our government's policy—these were the bastards who wounded Hernandez and Hecht and who killed and wounded many civilians the night before by indiscriminate . . . bombs. I could have killed the General and his orderly very easily—I have no conscience when it comes to these German soldiers.

This event must have occurred near General Patch's headquarters in Saint-Tropez, and Phil must have been attached at that point to headquarters.

The German general was most likely Ludwig Bieringer. He was captured on August 17 at Draguignan, a town north of Saint-Tropez, and brought to General Patch's headquarters on August 18. In my research, I found a picture of Bieringer in a jeep that is likely the one that Phil saw.[41]

Phil turned out to be wrong about the end of Bieringer's travels, for soon after his capture, he was sent to a POW camp in Mississippi and eventually moved to one in Arkansas. The United States envisioned using German officers to help in the de-Nazification process of other German POWs held in over five hundred POW camps spread across the United States and, at the end of the war, housing over four hundred thousand German and Italian POWs. All told, over three million German and Italian POWs were held in American camps here and in Europe.

Bieringer was the first of five German generals captured during those first days after the Dragoon landing. Soon after, Generals Ferdinand Neuling, Hans Schuberth, Kurt Badinski, and Erwin Menny were captured.[42] In his August 19 journal entry, Phil refers to another of his assignments at headquarters: "spent all afternoon hunting up a villa for our 3 German General guests. I'd [rather] tie lead weights on their necks and billet them in the bay."

The Dragoon landing contrasted greatly with the landing in Normandy two months earlier. On the Riviera, troops surprised the unprepared and undermanned Germans, quickly established their positions with relatively few casualties, and were ready to break out in pursuit of the retreating Germans within two days. In contrast, Normandy troops met fierce resistance, suffered huge losses before finally establishing their initial positions, and were not ready to break out and begin to liberate northern France until July 25, seven weeks after the June 6 invasion.

Up the Rhône Valley

Operation Dragoon had occurred so quickly and smoothly that troops were ready to "break out" from their initial foothold by the end of the day on August 16. General Patch had to decide whether to alter the original timeframe and immediately pursue the Germans who were rapidly retreating toward the Rhône River and up that valley. Patch ordered the pursuit, and the Sixth Army Group began to pursue the Germans at break-neck speed.

Phil, however, remained in the rear with headquarters, carrying out miscellaneous orders such as finding quarters for captured generals and interpreting French claims of American pillaging. Of these claimants, he says that their claims include "everything that they've lost or had stray or stolen since 1880" even though Americans have only been there six days. "The American is known as a real sucker the world over." Phil's small tasks keep him too busy to maintain his journal. His final eight days of entries are spread sporadically over a two-month period and almost all are short, such as these:

> [August 23] Yesterday ran about trying to locate PT boat
> and Blood Bank Plane. No cooperation from the Navy. US
> Navy man drunk around German prisoners, so I chewed him
> out—and threatened arrest.

> [September 4] I've become Mr. Fix-it. I get airplane rides
> for all nurses on rotation, Generals, Colonels, PFC ___
> who is returning to Naples to get married, PVT ___ who is
> returning to the U.S. to accept an appointment to Annapolis.

Soon journal entries are only jotted notes to help him recall events later: "Little kid & candy." "Colored boy drunk in gutter." But Phil described one incident in greater detail.

> [At breakfast] Lt. speaks of black market in Africa.
> Frenchman says that he can imagine—what with the Jews
> and Arabs in Africa what it is.
> I could hardly restrain myself from punching him in the

nose. I'm risking my neck for his country. I guess the French will turn out to be pretty much the same as people elsewhere. I could have told him something about his African black-market—about his noble and pure-blooded Frenchman who worked with our own noble and good American named officers.

No doubt anyone who read the journal would have felt the same way.

As Dragoon troops moved rapidly up the Rhône Valley chasing the Germans, Phil assumed his new courier duties, but he quickly tired of them. In a letter of September 19, he responds to an inquiry from Nathan:

> You ask what I am doing. Well, very little, but I'll try to give you an idea of my job. I'm a Courier—that means messenger boy . . . message to Garcia . . . and all that sort of stuff. If someone wants to tell someone else something, I carry the mail—documents, maps, reports, etc. There are about a dozen of us, minus the two fellows who got hit on D+1 (our only casualties). We travel by jeep, but our main duty is handling jobs by air. I'm sort of Chief Courier, so I dispatch the other fellows, keep records, reports, situation map, and do various odd jobs.

"Message to Garcia" refers to a well-known article by Elbert Hubbard published in 1899 and later made into a movie.[43] During the Spanish American War, President McKinley needed to communicate with Garcia, leader of the Cuban insurrection against Spain. Garcia was willing to help the Americans but was hiding somewhere in the jungles of Cuba. A soldier by the name of Rowan volunteered for the dangerous task of finding Garcia and delivering the message. The article turns Rowan's voluntary bravery into a metaphor for courageous, self-motivated employees who enthusiastically carry out their bosses' orders. The article ends with these words: "My heart goes out to the man who does his work when the 'boss' is away, as well as when he is at home . . . without asking any idiotic questions, and with no lurking intention of chucking it . . ., never gets 'laid off,' nor has to go on a strike for higher wages. Civilization is one long, anxious search for just such individuals. . . . The world cries out for such: he is needed and needed badly—the man who can 'Carry a Message to Garcia.'"

Phil reports doing "very little" but then tells this story:

> I grabbed a mail sack, went down to one of the airports and tried to get a ride back to Italy. An A-20 squadron was there and since I gave a couple of the lieutenants some K rations, they agreed to fly me down to the X____ airport. They didn't have any parachutes (for me) but whattha hell, I don't know how to use one anyhow. Besides they said that they'd make the trip "on the deck." And they did!! We raced along at 220 MPH. and skimmed trees and buildings. Along the R ____ River, we were 10 ft. from the surface of the water. We dived on bridges, roared over towns. . . .
>
> I unbuckled my safety belt threw open the hatch and stood up. . . . I was scarcely aware of the fact that the wind stripped my glasses right off my head. . . .
>
> We landed at a God-forsaken field, and I finally managed to get a ride to another field where . . . we got on a [C-47] . . . that took us to a town in Italy. We stayed overnight and the next day completed our mission.

The Unified Line

I think Phil's boredom was sincere. He was simply comparing his work with that of the front lines where he preferred to be. There, the Allies were advancing very quickly up the Rhône River Valley chasing the rapidly retreating Germans. In less than a month after landing on the French Riviera, the Sixth Army Group had advanced about four hundred miles and liberated Lyon, France's third largest city and a key transportation hub. In the process, they had suffered few casualties while inflicting many on the enemy and capturing over fifty thousand Germans.

The advance up the Rhône became known as the "Champagne Campaign," not simply because of the wineries filling the valley but because of the ease of advancement and the greetings troops got at each liberated town. Then, on September 10, the Dragoon troops made contact with the Normandy troops. It had taken the Normandy troops nearly three months to cover the same distance covered by Operation Dragoon in three weeks. The two armies now formed a north-south line through France, with the Twelfth Army Group in the north and the Sixth Army Group to its south.

The Germans continued to retreat to the Vosges Mountains to the east where they were regrouping and expected to take their stand. Some leaders in the Sixth Army Group were anxious to continue the pursuit and not let the Germans regroup or establish their defenses in the mountains, but there was a major problem. The front had moved much more quickly than its supply lines. For example, the After-Action Reports (AAR) of the 191st Tank Battalion on September 1 "expressed concern that long road marches and shortages of spares were forcing the battalion to continue using worn-out tracks [treads], and another tank battalion reported that its tracks would only last another two days."[44] The decision was to slow down for a week or so to obtain supplies and reestablish supply lines.

The Sixth Army Group paused in the vicinity of Épinal, France, while it repaired its tanks and replenished its supplies. It established a temporary burial ground that later became the permanent Épinal American Cemetery and Memorial. Among its 5,186 identified residents are most of the fallen soldiers who fought in battle with Phil. During this period between uniting in a single north-south line and fully resuming pursuit of the Germans, Eisenhower made several changes in leadership and troop assignments, and he gave General Devers and the Sixth Army Group substantial autonomy to accomplish two missions: "to protect the southern flank of Twelfth Army Group (the Normandy troops), and to destroy the enemy west of the Rhine, secure river crossings, and breach the Siegfried line."[45]

Somehow Eisenhower's orders left Phil without an assignment, for he was no longer characterizing his job as doing "very little" but as being "over." Here is how he reported this to his sister Jean in a letter of October 5, 1944:

> My job here has come to an end. It was another one of the
> many deals I've had where you work like mad, take risks
> . . . and then get sent off after a couple of months . . . thus
> adding a few months to your time in grade and getting you
> nowhere as far as promotion is concerned. In fact everyone
> begins to wonder what kind of a jerk you are (including
> yourself).

Reporting the same situation two days later to "Nate and Norm," he revealed that he has no idea what will happen next and is obviously struggling to accept whatever may happen:

> Well I'm through here and now I'm not sure what will
> happen. The Col. says he's going to send me to an Infantry
> outfit + 8 have already left. I may get a chance to go back
> with the fellows I used to be with in Italy. I really don't give
> a damn because as an armored Force Lt. I feel that when I
> get to the Infantry I can get hit hard enough to get home.
> One thing I'm sure of—I'll be a good platoon leader—or
> rather I'll try like hell. My fate is in the balance at the
> moment—I may go back or forward—and I'm ready for
> either. There are advantages to both. I'd welcome a chance to
> kill some Germans. I hate to do it in this kind of weather!!
> Oh well! C'est la guerre.

Phil was frustrated much as he had been prior to Dragoon. He felt he had not been used well by the army and that his initiative had been squashed at every turn. He felt guilty that he was not at the front risking his life like so many other soldiers. And he felt that he was spinning his wheels trying to be a good soldier and not being recognized for it. More to the point, he wanted a promotion to First Lieutenant, felt embarrassed that this hadn't happened, and was annoyed that he had been given assignments that didn't lead in this direction.

But, of course, the war didn't stop while Phil awaited reassignment. The Sixth Army Group resumed its attack on the Germans who, by now, were holed-up in the Vosges. To fulfill its new mission to "secure the river crossings and breach the Siegfried Line," the Sixth Army Group would first have to rout the Germans from the mountains. This proved to be very difficult in comparison with the relatively easy advance of the Champagne Campaign.

> By the first of October it had become apparent that the 45th Infantry Division was up against a strong enemy line. . . . The enemy was well dug in and appeared to be reinforcing his positions with little thought of the possibility of being forced to vacate them. Our rate of advance was retarded primarily because of the lack of local numerical superiority; . . . the fact that our troops were worn by long continued usage; and because of the characteristic German stubbornness.

Thus begins Maj. Dolvin's *Commander's Narrative for the Month of October, 1944 of the Activities of the 191st Tank Battalion.* By October 12, after fierce fighting, the 45th Infantry and its supportive tank platoons of the 191st had only been able to reach the area of Brovelieures, about ten miles northeast of Épinal. "For the succeeding week until October 21st, all the action in our sector was of a probing and holding nature, and even though we inflicted heavy casualties on enemy personnel, only very limited gains were made. Mines, bazooka fire and rugged terrain constituted the most troublesome opposition."[46]

It was during this period that Phil was reassigned to the front. He had not written at all in his journal for six weeks, but on October 16, 1944, he scribbled this entry:

> Reported to Major Dolvin C.O. 191st Tk. Bn. He was "glad to see me" and "needs me badly." Doesn't sound good. It's rough—woods.

He had gotten his new assignment.

10

At the Front

Doesn't sound good

Phil's quick assessment of his new assignment—"Doesn't sound good"—speaks volumes. He was acutely aware of several powerful realities crowded into that phrase—realities about battle casualties, Sherman tanks, and warfare in the Vosges Mountains.

Casualties

By fall 1944, the ground war in Europe had created major manpower shortages for the Allies and even more so for the Germans. Having depleted its pool of young men, Germany used some new methods. It dropped the requirement that foreign recruits to Hitler's special troops, the Waffen-SS, be Aryans; drafted women to serve behind the lines to free up men for battle; and drafted older men.[47] It also drafted men previously classified "unfit" and, for some reason, often placed them in units together. For example, in the Ardennes Offensive that led to the Battle of the Bulge, Germany used a unit of deaf soldiers and another of men with ulcers.[48] Increasingly, Germany sent recruits into combat with less training, returned wounded veterans to the rear or the front before they were fully healed, and provided less rest to their exhausted (and increasingly under-fed) troops.

The United States also needed new manpower approaches as the war progressed. Early on, we used women in industrial jobs (think of Rosie the Riveter) to free young men for the front, and soon after Pearl Harbor, we expanded draft registration to include men forty-five to sixty-five (Phil's father, Louis, registered on April 27, 1942, at the age of sixty-one). But manpower needs became particularly acute when we invaded Europe in 1944 and began to suffer heavy casualties. Consider this data: Annual casualties (troops killed or wounded) rose from about 4,000 in 1942, to 60,000 in 1943, to 479,000 in 1944. Until January 1943, monthly casualties never exceeded 2,500, but after that date they rarely fell below 10,000. Casualties exceeded 50,000 in most peak months of battle; and the highest months were the months in which Phil fought at the front—November and December 1944, and January 1945. In those months casualties were 66,000, 81,000, and 71,000 respectively.[49]

Eisenhower had many factors to juggle in designing the Allied effort in Europe—terrain, equipment, supply lines, leadership, and climate—but among the most complex was to figure out how to obtain and train the troops he would need. He knew that we were losing troops not only to death and injury, but also to capture, battle fatigue, and increasingly to desertion. He also knew, by mid-1944, of the dangers and limitations of merely looking to the draft for manpower. Anti-draft riots had just occurred in Canada where only half of the 16,000 draftees actually reported for duty. Americans also were increasingly restless over additional draft demands.

Ike began to expand manpower in unprecedented ways. He diverted troops to Europe that had been preparing for the Pacific, thinned supportive services, moved men to the front (Phil's situation), and increasingly assigned black troops to combat, even mixing them at times with white units that had been depleted. Hoping to stem the growing rate of desertion, Ike took the unprecedented step of refusing to commute the death sentence of a deserter. Eddie Slovak, "a poor little fellow from Detroit, brought up in the . . . great depression and incapable of adapting himself to army life," was shot on January 31, 1945, as a warning to other would-be deserters—the only soldier killed for desertion in World War II.[50]

M4A3 Sherman tank like Phil's, on display at Fort Knox

Sherman Tanks

As mentioned earlier, the United States was unprepared to fight when it declared war on Japan and Germany in December 1941. It had to act rapidly to obtain and train troops and to design and produce new weapons. Tanks were vital to the anticipated ground war. They would need to be versatile (able to perform in deserts and snowy mountains), fast and maneuverable (to serve in tandem with infantry units, a new assignment for armored divisions), easy to produce quickly (since we would need large numbers of them), readily transportable (we were fighting in very distant theaters of war), and able to stand up to German Tiger and Panther tanks (heavy tanks with enormous fire power).

The Sherman M4 tank in various models became the primary tank in the American arsenal. Phil trained in it, served in it, and would command his own M4 and a platoon of four or five others in the

191st. Shermans had many of the characteristics mentioned above. They were versatile, fast, maneuverable, and easily manufactured (over fifty thousand of them were produced) and transported. But Shermans also had some severe limitations and some vocal critics. One notable critic was Maj. Welborn G. Dolvin, Phil's new commanding officer. He had been in a tank and watched his shot bounce off a German tank before the return shot "went through the middle of Dolvin's tank, killing the driver instantly and setting the tank afire. Dolvin and the rest of the crew survived with serious burns."[51] Then in August 1944 he stated:

> The Sherman tank . . . is no match for . . . the German Mark IV, V, or VI. On numerous occasions, hits were obtained on German tanks with no noticeable results. On the other hand, German high-velocity tank guns never failed to penetrate the Sherman tank. This situation has a tremendous effect on the morale of the tank crews. This was evidenced by reluctance of crews to fire on German tanks, feeling that it would do no good and would result in their being promptly knocked out. Crews soon became ultracautious where German tanks were in the vicinity."[52]

World War II commentator Harry Yeide adds that "American tankers had been assured by the Army that they had the finest tank in the world, but it took only a few encounters—particularly with German Panther tanks—for them to realize they had problems." Another problem with Shermans, their flammability caused by the position of their ammunition storage unit, led the British to call them "Ronsons" after the cigarette lighter, and the Germans to call them "Tommycookers" ("Tommies" being a German name for British soldiers).

Vosges Mountain Warfare

The Vosges Mountains in northeast France lie in a north-south line from the Swiss border on the south to the German border on the north, bisecting a region known as Alsace-Lorraine. Lorraine lies on the west side of the Vosges while Alsace runs down the eastern slope of the mountains into the Rhine River Valley. Germany's well-known Black Forest forms the wall of the valley on the German side. In that sector, the Rhine forms the boundary between France and Germany. There are two sectors of the Vosges range, the High Mountains in the south and the Low Mountains in the north. The northern portion crosses the border into Germany. All of Phil's fighting was in the Vosges Mountains.

The Vosges have rounded peaks (in contrast to the Alps, for example) and are sometimes referred to as "The Blue Line" because of their blueberry covered meadows. But they are heavily wooded and receive much rain in the fall and much snow and cold temperatures in the winter. The winter of 1944–45 was particularly snowy and cold. The region has a rich history, partly evident in the remains of many remarkable abbeys and fortified castles in the mountains. It has been the site of much fighting over the centuries, and consists of two very different cultures, Lorraine, which is culturally French, and Alsace, which is culturally German.

For the Allies, the Vosges posed unique challenges, and fighting there gained its own designation, "Vosges Warfare." Yeide and Stout provide excerpts of the army's description:

> For the infantry, combat in the woods was in many ways comparable to jungle fighting. . . . Advancing in the woods, foot soldiers found the enemy allowed them to come up so close that friendly artillery could not be employed. Experiment proved it better to have a force in front of the main body to draw enemy fire. . . . The enemy was so well hidden that when he fired, only the general direction of his position could be located.[53]

At least when units were advancing—and that was the case much of the time as the Allies were pushing forward across France and Germany—the primary task of a tank each morning was to move forward in front of the infantry and "engage" the enemy. This deliberate effort to "get in harm's way" was especially dangerous because the enemy would select concealed, protected, and defensible

Heavy snowfall in the Vosges Mountains, 1944–45

positions at the end of the day where it could surprise attackers the next morning.

The army's description continues:

> The strain of hard fighting and the exposure to continuous rain and cold had their effects on the troops. Tree bursts from enemy artillery took a heavy toll and gave the men a certain feeling of helplessness. . . . Respiratory diseases, intestinal disorders, trench foot, and exhaustion cases increase, in some organizations more than double, during October. Trench foot in . . . the 3d Division increased from 54 in September to 160 in October to 448 in November. Armor could give the infantry only limited support. Tanks lost their maneuverability in the steep and wooded terrain of the Vosges and bogged down even on the shoulders of roads, softened by continuous rain. . . . Tanks were vulnerable to enemy rocket fire from concealed positions at close range and easily ambushed at night.[54]

Getting rations in harsh conditions in the Vosges Mountains, 1944–45

The difficulties of fighting offensively in the woods and mountains and in wet and then frigid conditions are revealed over and over in unit logs, as is the ferocity of the war.

Slowly North Through the Vosges

I began my search for Phil knowing only that he died somewhere in France. I wanted to know where, and now I knew. He died in the Vosges Mountains in the region of France known as Alsace-Lorraine. I knew this because Maj. Dolvin's 191st Tank Battalion was in the Vosges Mountains on October 16 when Phil joined it, and that unit remained in those mountains until March 1945, well after Phil's death on January 7. But the Vosges Mountains cover a large territory, and I felt there might be more to learn if I followed the progress of the 191st.

Quite in contrast to the Champagne Campaign in which the Allies, including the 191st, covered several hundred miles and reached Épinal in a month, fighting in the Vosges met fierce resistance, and progress was slow. For the 45th Infantry and units of the 191st Tank Battalion attached to it, simply getting to Bruyères from Épinal, a mere dozen miles, took several weeks. The Commander's Narrative Report tells us, for example, that on October 12, four days before Phil reported to the front, D Company "destroyed four more machine guns and assisted in the capture of 15 prisoners." By 5:00 p.m., it had advanced only about 700 yards when "the enemy launched a heavy counterattack [killing] a great number of foot troops." Company D and the infantry company to which it was attached "were forced to give ground."[55] As a result,

> For the succeeding week until October 21st, all the action
> in our sector was of a probing and holding nature, and even
> though we inflicted heavy casualties on enemy personnel,
> only very limited gains were made. Mines bazooka fire and
> rugged terrain constituted the most troublesome opposition.

The day after Phil reported for duty, he was shown around and made his final journal entry (October 17). It reads in full:

> 1st day. Out with Maj-Co. ____of the ____Bn of the ____ Reg.
> of the 45th Div. ____. Blurp gun, snipers, arty [artillery], etc.
> Plenty of Jerry equipment. Wounded pvt. taken by full col. to
> hosp. Met Lts. EM commissioned 5 days ago cracks. Surprised
> to see a man like that. Lt. 645th T. D. looks like hell.

Fierce fighting resumed on October 21 as the Allies, bolstered by several added divisions, went on the offensive. The Commander's Report says "The new offensive went well," but "well" didn't preclude a great deal of loss. Phil's C Company, for example,

> lost three tanks due to mines east of Fremifontaine and
> made only slight gains. At 0630 the next morning, October
> 23rd, the first platoon was in position overlooking the river
> (240643) and fired to cover the infantry in their crossing. One
> tank struck a mine when attempting to move down along the
> railroad track to take a hostile MG position under fire.

This type of action continued as the 45th Infantry and its attached tank units pushed their way slowly northeast through the Vosges.

"As the month drew to a close," Dolvin reported, "we were steadily approaching the reputedly strong Baccarat-Raon L'Etape-St. Die line." This was the last line of German defense south of the Saverne Gap, the gap between the High and Low Vosges Mountains that provided the Allies with access to the key city of Strasbourg, France, on the Rhine River across from Germany. By early November, United States and French troops had secured the Baccarat line. Then, "after fighting on the (front) line almost incessantly since landing in Southern France," the 191st was given a break. From the eighth to the twenty-second of November, recreation, rest, cleaning of equipment, the training of assistant drivers and assistant gunners, and defense against chemical attack were the important factors stressed on the training schedule.[56] During this period, the French First Army (the French component of the Sixth Army Group) moved through the Saverne Gap and secured Strasbourg. It would be a while before the Allies would cross the Rhine, but they were finally in sight of Germany.

The US Seventh Army (the American component of the Sixth Army Group), including the 45th Infantry supported by the 191st Tank Battalion, also headed into the Gap but turned north into the Low Vosges. By early December, they had moved near the German-French border that lies at the north end of the Vosges. Other Allied units also had moved close to that border and a competition arose for which unit would be the first into Germany. On the morning of December 15, Phil and his unit liberated the town of Petit Wingen, a mile south of the German border. Maj. Dolvin's Commander's Report from that day stated:

> This day, although comparatively meager in its scope of operations, should here be recorded and underscored; for early on the morning of the fifteenth, the 1st section, 1st platoon of Company "C" moved across the French border into Germany.[57]

This unit was among the first in the Sixth Army Group (the Dragoon

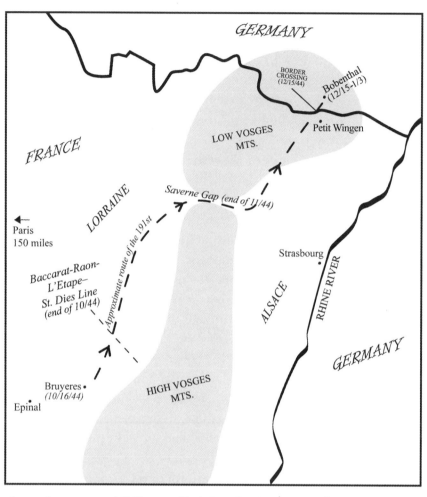

Approximate route of Phil's 191st Tank Battalion in Vosges to the German border,
October 16, 1944 to January 3, 1945

troops)—perhaps actually the first—to cross the French border into
Germany. An earlier crossing had been made by the Twelfth Army
Group (the Normandy troops) in September–October 1944 when it
crossed the Belgian border and captured the German city of Aachen.

The 1st section, 1st platoon of Company "C" was commanded
by Phillip Levy. Jack Del Monte was the feeder (the assistant gunner)
in Tank 2 immediately behind Phil's tank as they crossed the border.
At age ninety-three, he recalled the moment vividly and said he could

still hear Phil's voice on the tank intercom yelling, "We're first!" The event got headlines in *Stars and Stripes*, the army's newspaper:

Stars And Stripes, December 15, 1944

MAULDIN'S 45th BUDDIES AMONG FIRST INTO REICH
By ED CLARK (Stars and Stripes Staff Writer)
Germany, south of Kaiserslautern, December 15—
Company "K" Bill Mauldin's old outfit was among the leading elements of the 7th Army across the German frontier shortly after noon today.
The real winner of the closely contested race by Patch's doughfeet to the enemy border probably will never be known. Reports of time of frontier crossings by various units made the "first over" honors vary as crazily as early returns from a tight election. . . .
Rolling over the border with the doughfeet was "Chick," a big Sherman from Company "C" of a tank battalion. Commanded by 1st. Lt. Philip [*sic*] Levy, South Bend, Ind., "Chick" was ready to fire the first tank shell into the Siegfried Line. The crew included Cpl. Charles Williams, Old Hickory, Tenn., Pvt. John J. McHugh, Shenandoah, Pa., Cpl. Edward Paca, Delano, Calif., and Pfc. Ray E. Kelly, Eldorado Springs, Mo.[58]

Bill Mauldin, a sergeant with the 45th Infantry for much of the war, was well known for his cartoons with Willie and Joe, two gritty GIs fighting in the war. In 1945, he was awarded a Pulitzer Prize for these cartoons.

Of sixteen million American soldiers and additional millions of Allies in the war, Phil, who had served only two months on the front lines, happened to be one of the first across the pivotal French border into Germany! The moment certainly was the high point of his military experience, and two weeks later he finally had time to write home about it. He expressed his embarrassment that *Stars and Stripes* referred to him as "First" rather than "Second" Lieutenant, as much as he desired that promotion, and then his letter of January 2, 1945, stated modestly:

Dear Folks,
Here's an article that may be of interest to you. My tank was
the first in the 7th Army across the border. And I used to be
with 7th Army Rear!!!

Jeannie will receive a Nazi flag and arm band from the first
town taken by the first troops—in the first tank.
Love, Phil

Unfortunately, the family couldn't celebrate this remarkable
accomplishment, for by the time they received this letter, they had
learned of Phil's death.

MISHAWAKA NEWS 2/7/45   **The South**

SECTION TWO ★   SOUTH BEND, INDIANA, WEDNES

OPA TO HALT CAFE AB

The Lyons Den

BY LEONARD LYONS

A member of the plane crew which flew Henry Wallace to China tells this story of the trip: Just before they took off to fly over the Hump, oxygen masks were distributed, to all who were making the flight. Wallace spurned it. "You'll need it because we'll fly at such high altitude" . . . "No, I won't need it." Wallace insisted he would be able to withstand such needs by willpower alone" . . . The crew members shrugged, the plane took off and then each donned his mask. When the ship was over the Hump one crew member was sent back to see how Wallace was feeling. The vice-president was blue, groggy but still conscious. "Will you have a mask, sir?" he was asked . . . "Yes, thank you," said Wallace, and accepted it.

Group Capt. Owen Tudor of the RAF and his bride of a few hours flew from Washington to N. Y. for their honeymoon. Fiorello La-Guardia, whom they didn't know, approached them, learned they were honeymooning and volunteered to drive them to their hotel, the Madison. They were bewildered at first when they stepped into the mayor's car, which was waiting at the airport, and watched him lift a phone in the car and call his wife: "I'll be home in a few minutes" . . . Then Capt. Tudor told the mayor: "Our baggage. We forgot it" . . . "Baggage should not be the concern of honeymooners," LaGuardia assured them, "I'll send a police car for it" . . . The mayor drove them to the Madison. When they arrived they found that the police car, with their lost baggage, was waiting.

After 20 years of writing, Charles Rabner has his first

Lieut. Levy and Kovacevich Reported Killed in Europe

A former football player at Riley High school is reported killed in Luxembourg, and another well known South Bend soldier is listed as killed in France. Both had previously been reported missing in action. The names of three other local servicemen have been added to the list of those missing in action in France. They are:

Dead:
FIRST LIEUT. PHILLIP A. LEVY, aged 22, of 1518 East Colfax avenue; in France.
PFC. LOUIS J. KOVACEVICH, 21, of 2221 South Main street; in Luxembourg.

Missing:
Pfc. Albert R. Roscheck, 21, of 618 South Clinton street.
Private Sylvester E. Korpal, 28, of 1111 West Napier street.
Pfc. Irvin Worden, 20, of 1016 North Olive street.

Lieut. Levy, son of Mr. and Mrs. Louis Levy, 1518 East Colfax avenue, was killed Jan. 7. Going overseas with the tank battalion last October, he served in Africa and Italy and took part in the invasion of southern France. He was graduated from Central High school in 1937 and the University of Michigan at Ann Arbor before entering the service. Surviving besides his parents are his widow, Barbara, of Indianapolis; a brother, Nathan, South Bend city attorney; and two sisters, Mrs. Herman Seigel, at home, and Jean, attending the University of Michigan.

Private Kovacevich was killed Jan. 13. The son of Mr. and Mrs. Samuel L. Kovacevich, 2221 South Main street, he had been stationed overseas with the infantry since August, 1944. He was graduated from Riley High school in 1942, where he played left guard on the school's football team. He attended Butler university, Indianapolis, for a year and enlisted in the army in December, 1942, while still in school. He was called to active duty the following June. A member of the army specialized training program, he transferred to the infantry after that program was disbanded. Also surviving are three sisters, Yeoman 3/c Mrs. John Hartman, of Patuxent River, Md.; Mrs. Bert Schultz and Mrs. Howard Whiteman, of South Bend; and three brothers, George, Chris and Robert, at home.

Private Roscheck has been miss-

PHILLIP A. LEVY.

LOUIS J. KOVACEVICH.

LIFE SENTENCE GIVEN UNDER HABITUAL LAW

Jury Finds Sherman Guilty in Office Burglary.

Sylvester B. Sherman, a six-time loser in bouts with the law, lost another decision today and was sentenced by Superior Judge J. Elmer Peak to spend the rest of his life in Indiana state prison as an habitual criminal.

Sherman was found guilty Tuesday evening by a superior court jury which had listened for two days to evidence charging the defendant with burglary of the General Outdoor Advertising company office at 600 North Niles avenue, Nov. 28, 1944, and with habitual criminality. The jury deliberated only an hour and a half, convicting him on both counts.

Judge Peak, reviewing records showing that Sherman had been arrested 16 times and had served six penal terms in a crime career dating back to 1918, sentenced him to serve two to five years for second-degree burglary and then imposed the life term for habitual criminality.

"Your record does not speak in your favor, although you apparently never have used a weapon in your crimes," Judge Peak commented.

The judge pointed out that Sherman had contributed to the delinquency of a 12-year-old boy by taking the lad along in his car when he burglarized the advertising company. The boy testified against Sherman in court, as did two men who bought tires Sherman was accused of taking in the burglary.

Sherman, who is 40 years old, has resided at 132 South Wellington avenue. He is married.

PROMISED COLD WAVE DETOURS AROUND CITY

A cold wave heading this way has split and changed its course

Phil's death reported in *The South Bend Tribune*

II

Mystery at the Border

Ike said halt

The border crossing complicated my search, for it caused me to wonder how and why Phil ended up in France three weeks later. Had he simply been reassigned there sometime after the border crossing? Soon I found an answer, in several war history books and in an envelope from the National Archives.

The Ardennes Offensive

At the same time that the Sixth Army Group reached the German border to the south, the Twelfth Army Group had reached it in the north, having pushed through France and into Belgium. In its positions in Bobenthal, Germany, where Phil was stationed, and in other nearby towns, the Sixth Army Group awaited orders to push the Germans further into Germany. Instead, these plans were suddenly canceled. The reason was hinted at by Dolvin, now a Lt. Col., in his December report where he refers to "a large-scale enemy counter-attack [that] had begun on the 16th of December in the Twelfth Army Group sector."[59]

That German counterattack became known as the Ardennes Offensive, the next-to-last German offensive of the war. It occurred in the north against the Normandy troops and initially was quite successful. Eisenhower had expected this offensive but guessed wrong on where it would occur.[60] He hadn't expected the Germans to attack through the rugged Ardennes Mountains in the winter, and he left defenses in that region somewhat thin. As a result, the German offensive through the Ardennes initially pushed the Allies many miles back into France creating a large bulge in the line, and the ensuing battle became famously known as the Battle of the Bulge. It took weeks and heavy casualties for the Allies to eliminate this bulge.

Eisenhower faced a crucial choice as a result of the Ardennes Offensive. Should he allow the Sixth Army Group in the south to continue its promising advance into Germany, or should he halt it? He decided to halt the advance for two reasons: to keep a force in place that could protect the southern flank of the troops that were countering the bulge; and to prevent the possibility of the Sixth Army Group getting so far into Germany that it might become isolated, surrounded, or unable to maintain its supply lines without any chance of being rescued by troops now fully engaged in the Battle of the Bulge. The decision was controversial then and remains so today. One recent critic argues that the decision was not only wrong but was motivated by Ike's personal loathing for Sixth Army Group commander, General Devers.[61]

Following orders, the Sixth Army Group went on the defensive for the final weeks of December, strengthening their positions in the Vosges and trying to shore up their own line that ran along the mountain ridge for thirty miles from southwest of Wingen-sur-Moder, France, to the area of Bobenthal-Bundenthal-Niederschletterbach in Germany where Phil's unit was stationed.

Fighting continued along this line and, as always, Phil was careful not to alarm the home folks. Just a week before he was killed, he was upbeat and gossipy in a December 30 letter home:

> Tonight we made up some real chow. . . . I received a
> package from Aunts Pearl, Anne, and Faye. From it I took
> the sardines to be the appetizer. . . . Then we had soup which
> we made out of dehydrated meat and rice with water, onions

and a can of string beans with a pinch of salt. . . . And we
had green peas.

I wanted to do some letter-writing today, but I've been
rather busy. I went out on reconnaissance and then I hitch-
hiked to a shower unit and had a good, hot shower and a
change of clothes—the first since November 8th!!!

I'm doing OK too. I'm growing a mustache—just for
the heck of it. . . . Everything's going fine. I'm disgustingly
healthy. Love, Phil

But only a few days earlier, in a Christmas Day letter to his brother-
in-law, Sgt. Herman Siegel, Phil summarized his real experience. He
could open up with Herm who was serving stateside and could be
trusted not to share the letter with the rest of the family:

My life here is pretty rugged. It's colder than hell and the
tanks are like refrigerators—with ¼" of frost on the inside.
Just came back from inspecting my outposts. Nothing new.
Carried another GI back. Artillery barrage. Damn shame—
Christmas Eve too.

I've been "bazookaed," "Panzerfausted," hit mines, and
done everything a man can do. But I've been extremely lucky.
I've seen every type of combat—woods, city-fighting, river
crossing, etc. My last tank to be knocked out was hit by two
AP's—I can still smell the burning metal. Driver got his left
arm taken off and a hole straight through his right groin.
Ass't. driver badly beat up. The rest of us came out OK.

I'll be glad to see the end of this war.

As with the letter sharing news of his historic border crossing, this
letter would arrive after Phil was dead.

After invading Europe, there had been much hope among the
Allies that the war would end in 1944. Dolvin ended his "Year End
Narrative" by referring to this disappointment:

Those who had predicted that the war . . . would end in
1944 were proven wrong; all had hoped it would be; all
were disappointed. The officers and men of the 191st Tank

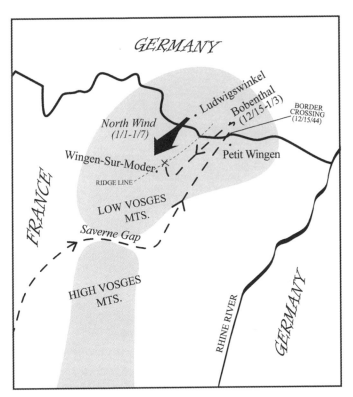

Approximate route of Phil's 191st Tank Battalion in Vosges
including return to Wingen-sur-Moder, January 3–7, 1945

Battalion who had [here he recites its accomplishments from
the invasion of Italy to this point], these men realized that
there was still alert [a lot of] hard fighting to be done in
1945.[62]

Dolvin added that, "Future plans seemed to depend, partially at least,
on what action was taken by the enemy."

The North Wind Offensive

In fact, Hitler was planning a very special action, and he timed it to
begin New Year's Day to add to the Allies' disappointment and to
stress that Germany was still strong and prepared to fight. Pleased by
the initial success of the Ardennes attack, he planned a companion

S E C R E T

Sheet No. 533(a) S-3 JOURNAL 191st Tank Bn

From __070001A Jan 45__ To __072400A Jan 45__

Place __Vicinity INGWILLER__

No.	DATE	TIME	INCIDENTS, MESSAGES, ORDERS, ETC.
	7 Jan		Cloudy & cold. Visibility: Fair.
		0810	Lt WARD telephoned Major HOLLIS regarding plans of 313th Inf to send tanks, inf and mine crew to mines in road found by Co D yesterday. Lt WARD stated they wanted a plat of medium tanks in addition to light tanks.
		0812	Major HOLLIS telephoned Capt KECK (S-3, 313th) informing him that the light tanks would be sufficient armor for operation.
		0820	Major HOLLIS telephoned Lt HENDERLY informing him of above mission. Lt HENDERLY was already informed and is sending Lt HOFFMAN's platoon.
		0900	Col DOLVIN telephoned Capt RPICE regarding keeping armor near PHILLIPSBURG until relieved by other armor.
		0920	Major HOLLIS telephoned Co A, 47th Tk Bn leaving instructions for CaptTHORPE to make plans for assembly of Co A in MUHLHAUSEN and to check with units before morning for relieving armor.
		0935	Col DOLVIN telephoned Capt COBB checking situation.
		0940	Major HOLLIS left for 313th Inf; 275th Inf; Co A, 25th Tk Bn; & Co A, 47th Tk Bn.
		0945	Col DOLVIN telephoned Capt WATSON (3rd Bn 179th) for situation.
		0950	Col DOLVIN telephoned Major QUILLO who reported PW report that enemy troops in WINGEN had pulled out with the PWs they held and reported one tank of this Bn bazookaed this A.M.
		1038	Capt COBB telephoned Col DOLVIN reporting Lt LEVY and entire crew KIA. Eny apparently thre grenade in turret. (This report erroneous).
		1050	Col DOLVIN left CP for Co C and 180th Inf Regt.
		1115	C.O., Co A, 47th Tk Bn telephoned asking for Major HOLLIS, was informed Major HOLLIS would be at Co A, 47th Tk Bn Hqs this A.M.
		1240	Lt MANZONE (179th Inf) telephoned reported one of forward cos reported they had taken Capt BERNHARDT away from an eny patrol.
		1310	Col DOLVIN telephoned reporting Capt BERNHARDT and Lt ST JOHN were with him and that he believes most of the E.M. escapted
		1455	Major HOLLIS back at CP.
		1505	Col DOLVIN back at CP with Capt BERNHARDT reported Co C tank hit by eny bazooka and by hand grenade. Lt LEVY and ass't gunner killed in action. 1 E.M. seriously wounded and 2 E.M. lightly wounded in action.
		1538	Received relayed message from 1st plat, Co A through

S E C R E T

The S-3 Journal report of January 7, 1945. The entry at 1038 was erroneous, as was the update at 1505. Only one crewman survived the attack.

attack in the south against the Sixth Army Group. He named it North Wind (*Nordwind*) and it would become the final German offensive of World War II.

The intent of North Wind was to push through the Allies' line in the Low Vosges, gain control of the Saverne Gap and the route to Strasbourg and the Rhine, and funnel troops and supplies through that Gap, pushing the Allies further back. When the Ardennes Offensive got stalled by late December, North Wind took on even greater significance and urgency in Hitler's mind.[63] He put an enthusiastic Heinrich Himmler in charge of North Wind, despite the fact that Himmler wasn't a soldier and had never directed troops. Himmler began to mobilize troops in Ludwigswinkel, Germany, only about six miles west of Bobenthal where Phil and his unit were stationed.

Among troops assigned to the operation were several elite troops including the 6th SS-Mountain Division that had been fighting the Russians for several years in the snow and mountains of northern Finland. The Finns had joined the Germans when Russia threatened to invade Finland, but suddenly on September 19, 1944, Finland entered into an armistice with the Soviets and agreed to disarm German forces remaining in Finland. Literally overnight, the Mountain Division was fighting its former ally and had to escape Finland. Its escape involved an arduous march of several months through the Arctic Circle and down the coast of Norway. Immediately upon completing this march, it was reassigned to Ludwigswinkel.

Wingen-sur-Moder

Soon after learning about the two German offensives, Ardennes and North Wind, I received responses to my military records inquiries. I was informed that Phil's personnel records were indeed among the sixteen to eighteen million veterans' records destroyed in the St. Louis fire, but I also received unit records of the 191st Tank Battalion from the National Archives and would obtain additional records from the Archives later.

I opened the envelope of unit records and was immediately amazed by their specificity. One set of records contained the daily log of communications with headquarters and set out the times and general content of each communiqué. I leafed through the January logs, looking without success for Phil's name until I got to the log for January 7, 1945:[64]

There it was. The official report of my uncle's death: "Lt LEVY and entire crew KIA." I felt as if I had just opened the dreaded War Department letter.

12

To the End

Behind me a tank is burning

After regaining my composure, I realized that the "0950" entry reported that Phil's unit was near a town named "Wingen." Suddenly I had a much more specific location of his death than I'd ever imagined I'd get. I Googled "Wingen" and learned that a major battle in the North Wind Offensive was fought there the first week of January 1945. We already ran into one Wingen, Petit Wingen, the town liberated by Phil and his troops on December 15 on their way to the German border about a mile away. But there are two towns called "Wingen" in this part of France, and the Battle of Wingen was fought in the second of these, Wingen-sur-Moder, about thirty miles southwest of Petit Wingen. I'll refer to Wingen-sur-Moder simply as "Wingen."

I began to read about the Battle of Wingen. It began on January 4, 1945, when veteran German troops overwhelmed Americans, mostly new recruits, who were defending Wingen. Many Americans were killed and more than two hundred were taken prisoner and held in the Catholic church. On January 5, the Americans began a counterattack with additional troops and regained some parts of the town. Fighting continued on January 6, but the American advance on the morning of January 7 met no resistance. They realized that all able-bodied Germans had escaped the night before, so they were able to secure Wingen without a fight. A picture from the battle shows a soldier approaching the Catholic church that held American POWs expecting to encounter enemy fire. Instead, he was suddenly surprised

US soldier approaches Catholic church to free prisoners, January 7, 1945

as the unguarded American prisoners came running out toward him.

This fact confused me. If there had been little fighting in Wingen on January 7, how had my uncle been killed there?

Seven Days in January

There is a great deal of literature on this battle and Operation North Wind; for example: *The Battle of Wingen-sur-Moder: Operation Nordwind*, by Wallace Cheves, commander of the Allied Forces at Wingen, and *The Other Battle of the Bulge: Operation Northwind*, by popular British military author Charles Whiting.[65] He called it "the other" because most of the attention at the time and since has been on the bulge created in the north by the Ardennes Offensive, but North Wind created a smaller and lesser-known bulge in the Vosges Mountains that also was critical to reverse.

My Googling provided me with a very interesting new lead, a book entitled *Seven Days in January*.[66] The book's "seven days"

Panoramic view of Battle of Wingen with Hotel Wenk burning in the background

were January 1 through 7, the last a day that of course had special significance to me. As it turns out, January 7 also had special significance to the book's author for he was captured that day and for him, as for Phil, the fighting ended. His name was Wolf Zoepf, and he was a commanding officer of the German troops at Wingen.

I went to Amazon.com, which allowed me to "look inside" at the beginning of the book. I read the opening line of the chapter entitled "Just Before Sunrise, 7 January 1945":

> The flickering light from the burning American tank behind me illuminated the otherwise seemingly pastoral scene to my front. . . .

I knew instantly whose tank was burning behind Wolf Zoepf. By then I had enough daily battle information from the S-3 journal to know that the 191st Tank Battalion lost only one tank on January 7—Phil's.

Immediately I ordered the book and it arrived a few days later. Its maps—Zoepf was an engineer and took great pride in the accuracy of his maps—located Company C of the 180th Division's 1st Battalion (the unit to which Phil's tank battalion was attached) on the ridge just north of town.

The book describes events chronologically so I turned immediately to January 6–7 and only later—from Zoepf's book and several other sources—read about events that led up to those days. Zoepf and his 6th SS Mountain unit had moved out of Ludwigswinkel, Germany, at 9:00 a.m. on New Year's Day and met no resistance as they crossed the border and stopped about five miles from Wingen. Then on January 2 and 3 they encountered Americans for the first time, having previously only confronted Russian soldiers in their several-year fight on the border of Finland.

Zoepf commented on some of the differences his unit encountered in fighting Americans in contrast to Russians. He noted that Americans seemed to use much more artillery prior to sending in the infantry, and he noted this particularly interesting contrast with respect to a battle the night of January 2–3:[67]

> In thirty minutes all hell broke loose! . . . After twenty minutes, I found myself taking cover in a ditch with [my men]. The Americans were pinning us down. With us in the ditch were the first dozen American prisoners, also seeking cover from their own mortars.

There was some advance of the Germans and then a rallying by Americans.

> It was close to midnight. . . . Someone from the American side called out in passable German, proposing a ten-minute cease fire to care for the wounded. Schultze [with Zoepf] agreed at once. The medics met in "No Man's Land," and evacuated the wounded to their respective sides.
>
> We were stunned. No event could have illustrated more clearly the difference between fighting the Americans and fighting the Russians, to whom such a truce would have been inconceivable.

Zoepf made other references to humanitarian acts of the Americans and the Germans, and he referred to joint humanitarian actions such as the joint aid station operated with German and American doctors and staffs.

Zoepf's unit was one of several German units that tried to attack towns lying below a thirty-mile-long ridgeline. American forces controlled most of that line, but there were several gaps, short intervals that were either held by Germans or that Germans had prevented the Americans from securing. Zoepf's Mountain Division was the only German unit to find one of these gaps. Its 750–800 men moved through the gap at night and down the mountain toward Wingen.

Early on the morning of January 4, it surprised the American defenders of Wingen, mostly new recruits in their first battle, and overwhelmed them. By noon the Mountain Division had cleared most of the houses in Wingen and placed prisoners in the church.[68]

The Americans responded quickly to the sudden loss. Already, anticipating a German offensive somewhere in the vicinity, they had begun to shift troops into the area. Some of the shifted troops took part in the Allied counterattack on Wingen that began January 5 and was led by a newly arrived commander, Major Wallace Cheves. Others, such as Phil's unit, were shifted and assigned to close gaps in the ridgeline north of Wingen. Phil's battalion was in Bobenthal at the far northeastern end of this thirty-mile ridgeline, and at 6:00 a.m. on January 3 it was detached from its infantry unit and quickly moved to Wimmenau, three miles from Wingen.[69] On January 4, it was reunited with its infantry division.[70]

After securing the road from Wimmenau to Wingen, the reunited tank and infantry units moved north toward the ridge to close a major gap in the line above Wingen—the gap through which Zoepf and his men had come. As the Americans moved north toward the gap, they could hear the Germans attacking Wingen, but kept on their mission to close the gap.[71]

By the end of the day on January 6, the 180th Infantry Division had closed the gap, but at a substantial loss. Company C—the company to which Phil's tank was attached—had suffered the worst.

Allies entering Wingen-sur-Moder, January 7, 1945

According to Zoepf who studied American reports in preparing his book, that unit reported sixty-four men remaining in the field—a fully-manned unit would have been 193 according to Zoepf—after five men were killed, fifteen wounded, and another seven "went to pieces [had nervous breakdowns]" in the fighting that day.[72]

Meanwhile, in town on January 4–5, Zoepf and his unit held back Americans and waited for the reinforcements they had been promised. Then on the night of January 5 a German messenger came through the same gap on the ridge that Zoepf had come through and gave Zoepf some bad news. There would be no reinforcements. Their new orders were to abandon Wingen.

The news was devastating to the Germans and left them with no option except to try a dangerous night escape. It was too near dawn on January 6 to leave, so the Division—exhausted, depleted, low on food, and low on ammunition—had to survive the pummeling by American artillery that day and then attempt their escape late that night. In his book Zoepf refers to this day as the "Inferno." At about midnight, those Germans who were physically fit gathered from house basements and other locations where they had been hiding, left the two hundred American POWs housed at the church unguarded, gathered at the railroad underpass on the east, and headed out of town. A heavy snow had begun that evening and continued through the night.

In Wingen on the morning of January 7, the Allies found that the Germans had escaped overnight, and took over the town without a fight. They released the American captives and celebrated their victory. The veteran Wallace Cheves, commander of most of the troops fighting in the town, surveyed the small town that morning:

Escaping German troops fled through this overpass in Wingen
on the night of January 6-7, 1945

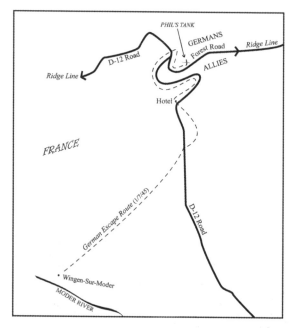

Escape route of Zoepf and German troops
on January 6–7, 1945

There were dead everywhere, men that I knew, stretched
out on the cold ground surrounded by Germans, frozen
in fantastic positions. There were other Americans [from
other divisions]. Everywhere I looked, in the middle of the
streets, in the ditches, in the buildings, on the embankments,
on steps, everywhere, there were dead frozen soldiers. I
never again saw so many dead together in one small area.
It seemed such a shame, and it was hard to realize that they
were actually dead, especially the ones I had known, the
ones I had talked with the day or so before. War had always
seemed so useless to me, and now it seemed even more
repugnantly futile.[73]

After bitter fighting and little sleep, the survivors had time only for
victory pictures before immediately being ordered to Puberg and their
next battle. Of those new orders, Cheves would report, "I couldn't
believe it."[74]

But I would not learn all of this background until after I read Zoepf's account of January 7. In small groups, the Germans made their way undetected to the railroad underpass leading out of town. From there they headed toward the ridge northeast of town and to the same gap they had originally found on their way to Wingen, the gap the messenger had come through the day before. They didn't realize that the gap had been closed after fierce fighting. The Charlie companies of the 180th Infantry Regiment and the 191st Tank Battalion, including Phil's platoon, had finally secured that small interval in the ridgeline.[75]

Zoepf and his men marched across country avoiding the roads and eventually came to the main road (the District Road, D-12). They stopped at 5:30 a.m. near the Kaminthaler Hof (Kaminthaler Hotel). At this point they figured they were "past all of the American defensive positions, and were in the middle of the no-man's land between [the Americans and Germans]." Their objective now was to climb up the road to the ridge and find German units on the other side. The hotel was closed so the Germans remained outside taking stock of their situation.

> . . . we took our first headcount (the two battalion total was:
> 9 officers and 217 enlisted men, fewer than a third of the
> 725 men who had begun the mission) . . . had a total of 360
> rounds [of machine gun ammunition], barely enough for five
> seconds' worth of fire per gun.[76]

The officers quickly set their strategy: They wanted to move forward swiftly with fewer than ninety minutes to early daylight. It was decided that Zoepf's battalion would lead the way since Zoepf knew the route well, having come through this area of the ridge on the way into Wingen. Around 0600 they left the hotel "marching single file up the district road. The remainder of the battalion followed some 300 to 400 meters behind followed by the other battalion."

Soon they came to the Forest Road that ran along the ridge. "The time was 0630," and Zoepf was toward the rear of his battalion.

As we rounded the bend, we perceived a dark, bulky object in the middle of the road; our lead element was just passing it, squeezing by on either side between the snowy boughs of the trees and the sides of the shape. Coming nearer, we discerned that it was a tank, and an American one at that. Its crew seemed to have been alerted by the passage of our men. We could hear the crew talking inside. Just then, Heuer and I noticed that the bow machine gun was taking aim on the men ahead of us, clearly lining up for a burst that could kill them all. We heaved our last hand grenade through the easily-opened hatch on the turret. Just as the last of the six scouts disappeared around the bend, Heuer and I jumped from the tank into the woods on either side of the vehicle, fearful that the detonation of our grenade would cause the tank's ammunition to go up any second.[77]

I was shaking as I read this passage, still shaking when I went downstairs and read it to my wife, and still shaking a few moments later when I called my sister to read the passage to her. I had begun my research with the hope of finding the general locality where my uncle had died. Now, I not only had found that answer. I also had found the ridge on which he died, the manner in which he was killed, and the name of the man who had killed him!

13

And Beyond

And so it goes

Had Phil survived, he and his buddies would have repulsed North Wind and won the battle for the Vosges. Then in March, with the 191st Tank Battalion still attached to the 45th Infantry Division, he would have begun the march through Germany to Munich. He would have arrived near Munich on April 29, 1945, and would have had a life-changing encounter.

Brigadier General Felix L. Sparks (retired), who was with the 45th Infantry Division, later summarized events leading up to that day:

> A day or so after the fall of Nurnberg [April 17, 1945], I was designated as a task force commander, with the mission of moving with all possible speed towards Munich, Germany. At that time, I was a lieutenant colonel commanding the Third Battalion, 157th Infantry Regiment, 45th Infantry Division, Seventh United States Army. Attached to my battalion for this mission were the entire 191st Tank Battalion.... We were able to smash through the sporadic German resistance with ease ... although the many blown bridges caused us some problems.[78]

On April 28, 1945, Sparks and his troops were fewer than thirty miles from Munich. After midnight he got his orders to resume the attack in the morning and enter Munich.

> I was also informed that the concentration camp near the
> city of Dachau would be in my attack area, but my orders
> did not include the taking of the camp. At that time, I
> knew virtually nothing about Dachau, except that it was a
> concentration camp near the city of Dachau.

Then as the attack resumed on April 29, Sparks received new
orders—to take the camp. Phil would have been part of the forces
that liberated Dachau.

In his recollection, Sparks described the camp.[79] Dachau was built
in 1933, the first forced labor camp to be called a concentration camp,
the first to use Waffen-SS guards, and the leading training ground for
future concentration camp commandants. Its first prisoners were two
hundred Communists who arrived on March 22, 1933. By then, Jews
internationally were well aware of growing German antisemitism. In
fact, Jews in America and Europe announced a boycott of German
goods on March 23, 1933, and twenty thousand Jews gathered at
New York City Hall that day and forty thousand at a rally at Madison
Square Garden four days later to protest Hitler's government. Hitler
responded in a speech on March 28, 1933:

> Lies and slander of positively hair-raising perversity are being
> launched about Germany. Horror stories of dismembered
> Jewish corpses, gouged out eyes and hacked off hands are
> circulating for the purpose of defaming the German Volk in
> the world for the second time, just as they had succeeded in
> doing once before in 1914.

Initially, any Jewish prisoners at Dachau were imprisoned for being
Communists and trade unionists, not Jews, but all of that changed
with the Kristallnacht arrests of November 9–10, 1938.

Sparks tells us that from outside Dachau looked like a typical
military garrison. Inside it had thirty-four wooden barracks for
prisoners and for kitchen, penal, and other functions. Each barrack
was designed to house 208 prisoners (but at the time of liberation,
each held 1,600 people). The camp was surrounded by high walls, with

Prisioners greet liberators of Dachau, April 29, 1945

SS personnel surrender to 45th Infantry Division at Dachau

guard houses in towers at each corner. Within the walls was a large confinement area surrounded by a moat and barbed wire fencing.

As he continued, Sparks described a preview that soldiers got before entering the camp:

> The first evidence of the horror to come was a string of about forty railway cars on a siding near the camp entrance. Each car was loaded with emaciated human corpses, both men and women. A hasty search by the stunned infantrymen revealed no signs of life among the hundreds of still bodies. Few words were spoken as the grim-faced soldiers deployed in battle formation towards the camp itself.

Later these cars were referred to as the "Death Train." Initially it was assumed that their corpses were Dachau prisoners who had been machine-gunned down by the SS, but actually the bodies were prisoners from Buchenwald who were being transported to Dachau.

Death Train at Dachau

Corpses in a Death Train boxcar

The train was delayed by American attacks on railways, and the prisoners were left for three days by the Germans to starve on the tracks outside the prison.

Jack Del Monte from Phil's platoon still pictured the Death Train vividly when we met in 2014. Because most bridges in the vicinity of Dachau had been blown up or were unstable, Jack's tank and others were delayed and missed the initial moments of Dachau's liberation, but as they neared the camp, they saw the boxcars. At first they thought they were simply filled with clothing, but then realized that the clothes were worn by corpses.

When Sparks reached Dachau, he noted the perverse words etched above the gate, *"Arbeit Macht Frei"* ("Work Sets You Free"). The gate was locked, so he and his troops scaled the walls and began to encounter the camp:

> The scene near the entrance to the confinement area numbed my senses. Dante's Inferno seemed pale compared to the real hell of Dachau. A row of small cement structures near the

Front page of *45th Division News*,
April 29, 1945

prison entrance contained a coal-fired crematorium, a gas
chamber, and rooms piled high with naked and emaciated
human corpses. As I turned to look over the prison yard with
unbelieving eyes, I saw a large number of dead inmates lying
where they had fallen in the last few hours or days before
our arrival. Since all the many bodies were in various stages
of decomposition, the stench of death was overpowering.

During the early period of our entry into the camp, a
number of Company I men, all battle hardened veterans,
became extremely distraught. Some cried, while others raged.
Some thirty minutes passed before I could restore order
and discipline. During that time, the over thirty thousand
camp prisoners still alive began to grasp the significance of
the events taking place. They streamed from their crowded
barracks by the hundreds and were soon pressing at the
confining barbed wire fence. They began to shout in unison,

which soon became a chilling roar. At the same time, several bodies were being tossed about and torn apart by hundreds of hands. I was told later that those being killed at that time were "informers." After about ten minutes of screaming and shouting, the prisoners quieted down.

The scene so angered some GIs that they machine-gunned down several SS officers who had surrendered. Most were simply shocked by what they saw and overwhelmed by the depth of inhumanity that obviously had been taking place there for a long time.

And almost all had another deep feeling that *The 45th Division News* of May 13, 1945, with its early story of the liberation, captured in its headline: "Dachau Gives Answer To Why We Fought."[80]

General Eisenhower had the same precise reaction upon seeing Ohrdruf, a sub-camp of Buchenwald, just after it was liberated on April 4. He ordered all American units in the vicinity to visit the camp, saying, "*We are told that the American soldier does not know what he is fighting for. Now, at least, he will know what he is fighting against.*"[81]

~

On May 8, 1945, just nine days after Dachau was liberated, the war in Europe ended, and several months later the whole war ended with the Japanese surrender on August 15. The 191st remained in Hohenkammer, a few miles north of Munich, until it was deactivated in August.

In his farewell to the 191st, Lt. Col. Dolvin spoke about heroes, and his remarks led me to wonder about Phil's heroism. Of course, in the popular view, Phil and all other World War II soldiers in good standing are heroes—whether they enlisted or were drafted, joined out of an itch to fight or a long family tradition or some deep sense of commitment; whether they acted bravely or cowardly, served at the front or the rear, soldiered-through or fell to pieces, killed their enemy or negligently killed their allies; whether they survived or died. In turn, we honor them in innumerable ways—ticker-tape parades, flag-draped coffins, VE and VJ and Memorial days, fly-overs at sports events, metal grave markers—and we deem them "The Greatest Generation."

From among these heroes, the army automatically singles out those who put their lives on the line and died or were seriously injured in action.[82] It awards them Purple Hearts, and Phil qualified for his by meeting the most common criterion, being killed in action. Elsewhere I mentioned that Sherman tanks like Phil's were called "Ronsons" by the Brits and "Tommy-cookers" by the Germans. But to American tank men, they were called "Purple Heart boxes."

Dolvin, bidding farewell to the 191st in August 1945, focused on another category of heroes, those who perform special acts of bravery. Some in this category are recognized for their bravery, and Dolvin himself became one of the most highly decorated soldiers ever, ranking 47th (using a scale based on points for various medals) just behind General Norman Schwartzkopf on a list headed by General Douglas MacArthur.[83]

Others who act with special bravery, however, are never officially rewarded, and Dolvin chose to recognize these unsung heroes in his final remarks:

> Today . . . I am not going to single out and talk about any particular heroes. The recognized heroes have their memorials engraved upon records, silver and bronze. Today, I want to talk primarily about a type of soldier whose deeds were not recorded—the fellow who stayed with the tank to the end and who fought against superior odds to the best of his ability—but who, unfortunately, did not have any witnesses to his last stand. . . . I shall call my subject: "Unknown Private John Smith."
>
> Yes, you know him and I know him. We saw him all along the way—that is, until he left us. . . . There are many of his kind before me today. He was at Lexington pitifully armed. . . . He was at Bunker Hill, Saratoga and Yorktown. He was at . . . [Dolvin refers to Anzio and other battles engaged in specifically by the 191st].
>
> Private John Smith may not have been the name of the

unknown hero. . . . His name may have been O'Flaherty—it may have been Bernowsky [*sic*]—it may have been Capelli—it may have been Cohen, it may have been Chavez—and it may have been Schmitt. Whatever it was, it is a certainty that so long as there are "Private John Smiths," "Private Rusek Barowskys" [*sic*], Private Mike Capellis, Private Bennie Cohens, Private Juan Chavez and Private Otto Schmitts, in America, our country's future is assured to be a good one.[84]

Surely Phil Levy was in the minds of some in the crowd that day, perhaps even the speaker's.

~

At war's end, it certainly is fitting—comforting, reaffirming—to recall the virtue of our cause and the heroism of our fighters. Dachau and Dolvin provided this opportunity to the 191st. I wish Phil had witnessed the official end of the war and been there for Dolvin's speech; and even more so, I wish he could have helped liberate Dachau, for it would have confirmed his measured decision made six years earlier to join the military and fight.

But as we all reluctantly realize, virtue and heroism are only half of war's ledger. The ledger's second column is death and an array of other wartime casualties. It provides a constant reminder that war is hell and that its fighters are simultaneously heroic and tragic. As citizens of a democracy, it is vital to keep the full ledger in mind, for wars are human choices, not accidents of nature. Our sacred duty, owed perhaps mostly to youth, is to make our war choices wisely. Full ledgers, honest information, and open public dialogue are essential to this duty. If we allow comforting declarations of virtue and heroism—even the most valid of them—to overwhelm or minimize the other half of the ledger, we do so at great peril.

In the limited context of my personal search for Phil, ignoring the full ledger would rob his death of the paradoxical meaning it deserves. So here is my summary of the ledger's other column. Phil was among the 405,000 American soldiers killed. Another 700,000 were wounded. Massive as this seems, it is small compared to the sixty million soldiers and civilians killed worldwide. Our ally, the Soviet Union, lost 14 percent of its entire population and other nations had comparable losses. Most of the Jewish population in German-occupied countries were killed, about six million in all.[85] Millions more were maimed and additional millions who lived in war zones were raped, starved, and/or imprisoned. The estimated cost to the United States alone—and we, of course, suffered very limited civilian loss or damage to homes, businesses, farms and other property—was over $4 trillion in today's dollars.[86] The costs around the world were many times this figure. And, of course, these are only the computable price tags of war. Equally vital costs arose from the hideous impact the war had on our families and on our individual and collective hearts and souls.

Slaughterhouse Five[87] was a particularly powerful reminder of the horror of war and one of America's great novels, ranking seventeenth on the Modern Libraries list of the one hundred best novels of the twentieth century.[88] It was written by Kurt Vonnegut whom you may recall was Barbara's childhood neighbor and classmate, and was based on his own deeply distressing experience in World War II. The experience was, in fact, so traumatic for Vonnegut that he was unable to complete the book until 1969.

In considerable contrast to the experience of the liberators of Dachau, Vonnegut's war led him to the Battle of the Bulge where he was captured and sent to Dresden. As a POW, he was held by the Germans in an old Dresden slaughterhouse and was there on February 13–15, 1945, during the infamous fire bombing of that city by American and British airmen. Dresden, the center of German culture and known as the "Florence of the Elbe" was leveled. Vonnegut was ordered to help collect and bury the bodies of the twenty-five thousand victims of the bombing, mostly civilians. That number is two or three times the Allied fatalities on D-Day at Normandy.

There is much controversy about whether the bombing had any strategic value to the Allies at that point in the war, and Vonnegut was among those who felt it was purely vindictive and immoral. In an introduction to a tenth anniversary edition of the book,

Vonnegut wrote, "The Dresden atrocity, tremendously expensive and meticulously planned, was so meaningless, finally, that only one person on the entire planet got any benefit from it. I am that person. I wrote this book, which earned a lot of money for me. . . . Some business I'm in."

Slaughterhouse Five tells the story of Billy Pilgrim, a fictional character who has the same war experiences as Vonnegut. Billy goes to fight as a young boy in the Battle of the Bulge. Early in the chaotic battle, he and some buddies get lost, are captured, and are marched and transported by boxcar to Dresden where they are imprisoned in Slaughterhouse Five, an old meat plant. Thanks to the thick-walled plant, they survive the firebombing of Dresden and are required by their captors to help bury the dead. Here, the literal resemblance of the experiences of Billy and Vonnegut ends, for unlike Vonnegut, Billy suffers a mental breakdown that persists when he gets home. He becomes "unstuck" in time, and time-travels to various events in his life, past and future. As if confined by fate, however, Billy is able only to observe, not to alter, these events. "So it goes," observes Vonnegut over and over, in the book's hallmark phrase.

Perhaps the most poignant event of the novel occurs in its non-fictional introduction. Vonnegut is visiting a war buddy, Bernard O'Hare, twenty years after the war and after he has begun to write *Slaughterhouse Five*. While Bernard and Kurt sit in the kitchen, Bernard's wife, Mary, pops in and out, obviously very upset with Vonnegut. He has no idea why:

> I asked O'Hare what I'd said or done to make her act this way.
> "It's all right," he said. "Don't worry about it. It doesn't have anything to do with you." That was kind of him. He was lying. It had everything to do with me. . . .

At a point, Mary returned to the kitchen and

> let me see how angry she was, and that the anger was for me. She had been talking to herself, so what she said was

a fragment of a much larger conversation. "You were just *babies* then!" she said.

"What?" I said.

"You were just babies in the war—like the ones upstairs! (the O'Hares had two children sleeping upstairs). . . . But you're not going to write it that way, are you." This wasn't a question. It was an accusation.

"I—I don't know," I said.

"Well, *I* know," she said. "You'll pretend you were men instead of babies, and you'll be played in the movies by Frank Sinatra and John Wayne or some of those other glamorous, war-loving, dirty old men. And war will look just wonderful, so we'll have a lot more of them. And they'll be fought by babies like the babies upstairs."

So then I understood. It was war that made her so angry. She didn't want her babies or anybody else's babies killed in wars. And she thought wars were partly encouraged by books and movies. . . .

So . . . I made her a promise. "Mary," I said. ". . . If I ever do finish [this book], I give you my word of honor there won't be a part for Frank Sinatra or John Wayne."

This incident so influenced Vonnegut that he dedicated the book to Mary.

Vonnegut's theme of the soldier as victim rather than hero struck a chord with many in the Vietnam era, including myself. Our leaders entered, expanded, and prolonged that war through dishonesty and deception that hid the full ledger from us and prevented the type of open and informed dialogue needed in democracies where citizens influence grants of war powers, declarations and escalations of war, resumptions of the draft, and allocations of funds to defense and diplomacy. They sent boys to war who, like Billy, were simply answering their country's call and doing their duty, with little sense of what they were fighting for or against, or of how hellish war can be. And most of us tolerated or even hailed these events without realizing or demanding the truth and the full ledger.

So Vietnam provoked a different vision of heroism. In it, the traditional soldier who automatically answered his country's call and even the brave warrior became tragic rather than heroic figures. At that moment in time, we began to define heroes as those who demand explanations for war and oppose it or refuse to fight until those explanations are honestly provided. Heroes were those who insisted on weighing the hell of war against its proclaimed virtues and only then choosing to fight or resist, support or oppose the war.

So I particularly envision my uncle as a hero. He was a hero in the traditional sense—answering the call, putting his life on the line, maybe even exhibiting distinctive bravery. But he also was a hero because he made a carefully measured choice. He studied the necessity for this war and opted to fight in it long before it was popular and long before the United States declared war. Even "while most of [his] fellows were holding peace rallies," he concluded that war was the only way to stop Nazi injustice and that the value of waging war outweighed its horror and the risk of death. In this sense, he was an especially notable hero to me, and it is for this reason that I so wish he had gotten to Dachau.

But his death is also notably tragic. The following description of Allied strategy late in the war underscores the tragedy. Toward the end, the war became a war of human attrition fought in the Ardennes and Alsace. Quite simply, by then "the Allied losses could be replaced, the German casualties could not."[89] So, as historian Roger Cirillo states:

> Hitler spent his last reserves in Alsace and with them the ability to regain the initiative anywhere. Like the Normandy Campaign, the Ardennes-Alsace struggle provided the necessary attrition for the mobile operations that would end the war. The carefully husbanded enemy reserves that the Allies expected to meet in their final offensive into Germany had been destroyed in December and January.[90]

In brutal terms, Phil could be replaced, but Franz could not. If we sacrificed a Phil for every Franz, we would prevail—and, all too literally, that's exactly how we won.

14

Nuremberg, Zoepf, and Voss

A thoroughly decent man

The war trials at Nuremberg began on November 20, 1945, a half-year after the war in Europe ended. Phil, likely en route to law school after the war, would have followed the trials closely. Initially, the International Military Tribunal tried individual defendants. Judgments were handed down in the fall of 1946, and on October 16 ten defendants were hanged using the standard drop rather than the long drop method, a choice that seemed to make death agonizingly slow for several of them.

On July 30, 1946, the trials of criminal organizations began, including the trial of the SS (Schutzstaffel). The SS began as Hitler's special forces and became the international militia of Nazi Germany, separate from Germany's regular army, the Wehrmacht. On October 1, the Tribunal handed down its judgment that the SS and "persons who had been officially accepted as members of the SS" were criminals, and attributed a broad range of atrocities to them:

> [The SS] supplied personnel for the Einsatzgruppen [the death squads that committed many mass murders] and had command over the concentration camp guards . . . was widely used in the atrocities in occupied countries and the extermination of Jews there . . . [and] was responsible for such special projects as the human experiments and 'final solution' of the Jewish question.[91]

It reasoned that these activities "followed quite logically from the principles on which [the SS] was organized . . . the ultimate domination of Europe and the elimination of all inferior races." Finding it "impossible to single out any one branch of the SS which was not involved in these criminal activities," the Tribunal delivered its guilty decree that reached all members of the SS, including Wolf Zoepf and the men of his 6th SS Mountain Division.[92]

Anger toward Wolf Zoepf wasn't among the feelings that overwhelmed me when I came upon his description of events on the Forest Road. After all, it was war and he merely did to Phil what Phil was about to do to Zoepf's men. Eventually it was curiosity rather than animosity that led me to want to know more about him, and that curiosity was particularly propelled by the way he is characterized in the introductory material to *Seven Days in January*.

The book's preface is by US Brigadier General Theodore Mataxis who fought in the Vosges and later met Zoepf at one of several joint gatherings of American and German veterans of the Battle of Wingen. He notes that both he and Zoepf were second in command of like-sized battalions at ages much younger than the norm for holding those positions. After describing joint reunions as the best path to reconciliation of nations after war, Mataxis praises Zoepf for being instrumental in organizing the Wingen gatherings.

He also cites two humanitarian actions of the SS under Zoepf at Wingen: the humane treatment of prisoners captured by that unit, and the operation of the joint medical aid station where SS and allied doctors triaged soldiers based on wounds and not nationality. He saw these as "amazing example(s) of chivalry in a war otherwise often known for its pure ferocity and inhumanity" and reminded readers of the massacre of eighty-four American POWs by other SS and Luftwaffe troops just a few weeks before the Battle of Wingen and only a few miles away in Malmady, Belgium.

In an editor's note in Zoepf's book, Keith Bonn expands on Zoepf's humanitarianism. He got to know Zoepf while editing the book, and gained respect for "his formidable intellect; his straightforward and soldierly candor; his clear memory of details. . . ." He refers to Zoepf as a "fine soldier and [a] considerate, thoroughly decent man."

Thoroughly decent? This isn't an attribute of anyone in the extensive rogues' gallery of the SS or in the judgments handed down at Nuremberg. Nor is it my perception of the SS. I have seen them as a pack of elite soldiers dedicated to the Nazi belief of Aryan racial superiority and responsible for committing a wide range of atrocities, particularly actions of racial and ethnic cleansing generally and extermination of Jews in particular. And I have seen the same SS pack as unapologetic and unrepentant after the war. Perhaps tributes to Zoepf's decency were intended narrowly to apply only to his chivalry in war, but I took them to be much broader. I took them to suggest that Zoepf somehow contradicted the customary SS stereotype that I also held.

Sweeping generalities about groups of people are rarely accurate. Not only do I believe this, but I have devoted considerable parts of my life work to dispelling such stereotypes—of women, of people with disabilities, of African Americans, of welfare recipients and of poor people generally—and sought to reveal faces that are hidden by such broad brushes. I also believe that people who hold stereotypes can change their beliefs and attitudes. Personal stories can be a key way to dispel over-generalizations. Stories of individual lives have the power to confront such broad brushes as "illegal aliens," "lazy, cheating welfare recipients," "defectives," and "felons," and uncover the complex human being lurking under the generality.

Since I'm not immune to stereotyping, I welcomed an opportunity to explore my broad-brush vision of Waffen-SS soldiers, and I wondered if the story of a "thoroughly decent" SS officer named Wolf Zoepf—perhaps a humanitarian rather than a miniature Heinrich Himmler or Joseph Mengele—might help me test my stereotype. Was he thoroughly immersed in Nazi ideology and antisemitism when he joined the SS? Did his views change substantially after the war? Off the highway I raced to learn his story.

Zoepf's Resumé

From several sources, I assembled a rudimentary portrait of Zoepf. He was born in Riga, Latvia, in 1922, the same year Phil was born.

Wolf Zoepf as a twenty-year-old officer in SS-Nord

His family owned a bookstore there. They were "Baltic Germans," Germans who had moved to the Baltic States years earlier, in some cases hundreds of years earlier. Though a minority in the Baltics, Baltic Germans had become a proud political and economic elite.

In 1939, Russia was poised to invade neutral Latvia, and Baltic Germans would have been among its early victims. To avoid war with Russia, Hitler secretly agreed to let Stalin capture the Baltics, but first he invited Baltic Germans to return to the motherland. Behind this offer were two hidden motives. Hitler needed Baltic Germans and other ethnic Germans (Germans living outside Germany) to fill the ranks of the SS. He also needed them to inhabit nations to the east that Germany was conquering and to transfuse those populations with "superior" ethnic stock. Baltic Germans were the initial group in this resettlement initiative (which, incidentally, was operated by Heinrich Himmler) and most were placed in Poland. Many Latvians were unaware of this resettlement plan and expected to return eventually to Latvia. They were extremely disturbed when Hitler refused to let them go home after Germany conquered Latvia in July 1941. Hitler's plan spelled the end for the long-cohesive Baltic German ethnic group. Once scattered, it never again was able to coalesce.[93] I don't know whether Zoepf's family was placed in Poland or simply returned to Germany.

In 1940 on his eighteenth birthday, Zoepf enlisted in the SS. He fought with the 6th SS Mountain Division until his capture in 1945. In 1943, he attended Officers' Training at the famous Junkerschule at Tölz, Germany, and became an officer. Most of his fighting was with the Finns against the Russians in northern Finland until the Finns signed a non-aggression treaty with Russia, joined the Allies, and promised to rid their nation of German soldiers. As I mentioned

Wolf Zoepf on right at January 6, 1990, gathering of German and American
Wingen veterans at Las Vegas reunion

earlier, to escape Finland Zoepf and his men made their way back to
Germany by hiking for two frigid months, mostly through the Arctic
Circle and along the coast of Norway. Upon their return to Germany,
they were immediately reassigned to Operation North Wind where
Zoepf served for seven days until his capture on January 7, 1945. He
was a POW in an American camp in Europe until the spring of 1946
and returned home to a family that had assumed he had been killed.

Zoepf married his childhood sweetheart, Ruth, whose family
had been Baltic Germans in Latvia for over four hundred years.
They had several children. Wolf obtained an engineering degree
and practiced civil engineering, doing extensive work in Africa and
Asia. In 1992, he co-founded Domus Rigensis, a German-Latvian
cultural organization in which he served as an officer.[94] He also was
active with the Mountain Division veterans' group and the German
War Graves Council. He was instrumental in arranging the "highly
controversial" joint reunions of American and German veterans

of the Battle of Wingen, and was made an honorary Trailblazer, a member of the US Army's 70th Infantry Division.

In 1999, he wrote *Seven Days in January*, and it was published soon after he died. The well-written book is primarily an account of the Battle of Wingen and details both German and Allied strategies and action associated with that battle. It is carefully researched, often drawing on Allied documents. Zoepf read detailed daily records of Allied units including those of the infantry unit to which Phil's tank was attached. He read materials written by Wallace Cheves who led the American counterattack against Zoepf, and wrote to Cheves and spoke with him on several occasions. He worked hard to verify his recollections and to draw accurate, detailed, daily maps of the battle. Various commentators have complimented the book as a very balanced account.

The book is a military treatise and offers little insight into Zoepf's beliefs. It demonstrates his longstanding interest in military matters, his pride in being a soldier, and his commitment to his men. I suspect it is this last matter that led the United States publisher, Aberjona Press, to print his book. Aberjona founder, Keith Bonn, was a West Point graduate and army veteran who later earned a PhD at the University of Chicago working under Edward Shils and Morris Janowitz. His two professors were well known for seminal research that showed that soldiers might go to war for many reasons, but they fight primarily to fulfill a bond to fellow unit members, what the researchers termed "primary group solidarity." Bonn continued this research by studying World War II battles in the Vosges Mountains,[95] and then established Aberjona to publish books that further explore or illustrate the theme of primary group solidarity. Zoepf's book illustrates this theme vividly.

My information produced an interesting resumé for Wolf Zoepf but few clues to his motivation for joining the SS, his wartime beliefs, or changes he might have made in those beliefs after the war. In a last effort to get beyond a resumé, I got in touch with Aberjona. Keith Bonn had died and his wife Patti was now editor. Unfortunately she had had very little contact with Wolf Zoepf and had little to tell me about him, but she tried to help. She provided this interesting anecdote. Zoepf died just after he and Aberjona completed the book but before it was released. Keith Bonn went to his funeral. When he met Zoepf's widow and son there, he asked how they wanted to handle the book. "What book?" was their response. Such mysterious and complicated things, those family silences! She also relayed a request by me to Zoepf's son to see if he would be willing to speak with me about his father. He wasn't.

Patti also referred me to another Aberjona book, *Black Edelweiss*, by Johann Voss (a pseudonym).[96] Voss served with Zoepf in the 6th SS Mountain Division and knew him after the war. After I read the book, Patti helped me contact Voss. At the age of about ninety, he responded politely to my inquiry, providing a few windows into Zoepf's beliefs. The most interesting was this:

> My relationship with Zoepf wasn't a close friendship. It couldn't be, given the rare occasions we were together. But certainly did we esteem each other. During our trips to Karelia [in Finland where they had fought the Russians]— after the breakdown of the Soviet Union—it showed that we shared many political views, particularly regarding the extinction of the European Jews and the disgrace the lunatic fringe of the German leadership has brought upon our people. His rich professional life abroad taught him to take an objective view on our country and countrymen, for all the patriotic feelings both of us shared. [97]

With only a few relevant bits of information, my search for a Zoepf story that might change my SS stereotypes had reached a dead end.

Voss's Story

Johann Voss's story, however, turned out to be much more promising. Rather than a military treatise, it is a deeply personal story of regret, introspection, and personal growth. Though published in 2002, it is essentially a journal that Voss kept while he was a prisoner during 1945–46 in an American POW camp. He was seventeen when he joined the SS and nineteen when he was captured near the end of the war, one of only two men in his unit to survive its final battle. He felt writing the journal and eventual book was a genuine way to give a voice to many of his fellow soldiers who did not survive the war but who would have had similar life stories to reflect on afterwards.

In the book he tries to understand how he could have been so wrong in his commitment to the Reich and become so implicated in a system of atrocity. In the POW camp, he began to learn of the atrocities committed by soldiers wearing the SS uniform:

> Since we came here in May . . . reports of large-scale atrocities and mass killings kept coming in. . . . There were rumors at first, then more and more newspaper articles, and, in particular, pictures of concentration camps liberated in the course of the defeat, horrible photographs gazed at in disbelief by the prisoners of war; human beings, nearly or definitely starved to death, hundreds of them. . . . In the agonizing hours, especially at night, when haunted by those pictures, I realize all these people have been held in the custody of men who wore the uniform I wore myself. . . . [98]

Throughout, Voss struggles with his feelings and tries to understand his actions. For example, he writes at length of regrets at not listening more carefully to his parents and family—his father who had reservations about Hitler and the SS, an uncle from Sweden who mocked Hitler, and his parents who "found Hitler's hate of the Jews repulsive." But complicating this was the fact that Voss's sister was an ardent Nazi and another uncle was an aide to a major Nazi official. He reports extensively on key interactions with each of these family members.

He reflects back on clues of Nazi persecution that he had earlier ignored or discounted. One particularly chilling incident is described in a chapter entitled, "A Glimpse Into An Abyss." As he and his Waffen-SS unit were being transported to the Russian front and their first combat, their train stopped and Voss saw twenty or thirty men laboring in a repair crew.

> I saw the faces of the gang. . . . Horror struck me. Large
> black eyes in deep eye sockets, imploring and frightened,
> stared from pale, emaciated faces under woolen peaked caps
> that looked ridiculously large. Most of them wore the yellow,
> six-pointed Star of David on their jackets. I shivered as I
> watched them lift their hands to us and timidly shout, "Mr.
> soldier, sir, a piece of bread, please."[99]

A soldier in the next car handed a youngster a half-loaf of bread, which the child hid, but another prisoner dragged the child to a guard who demanded the bread and then kicked the youngster and beat him with a rifle. All the SS soldiers on the train started yelling to stop and their superior officer, von Hartmann, leaped from the train and ordered the guard to stop. The guard momentarily confronted von Hartmann but relented, and von Hartmann and an assistant took the boy to a local authority (the assistant later reported that the commander made a report and was promised that the boy would not be assigned to the same labor unit). Von Hartmann returned to the train and it moved forward.

Later when von Hartmann visited Voss' train car and asked how everyone was doing, Voss had a chance to say, "We were relieved when you intervened in the incident this morning." Von Hartmann's face became stern; only his eyes showed that he appreciated what was implied. "It was a severe offense against discipline," he said. ". . . It's the duty of everyone to see that discipline is restored on the spot."

Voss was aware that he had witnessed an example of Jewish persecution, not merely excessive punishment of Jewish criminals; at the time he played it down. He realized that certain things would have to change after the war but first the war must be won. Seventeen and on his way to his first combat, he quickly turned his mind back to the task at hand. However, as he recalled the incident during his internment in the POW camp, he wondered why he hadn't sensed the large scope of atrocities that the incident suggested. Günter Grass in *Peeling the Onion,* ended with the same consternation, wondering how he could have been so meek and non-inquisitive with respect to multiple, small glimpses he had as a teenager into the same abyss.

Voss regretted what he considered his impulsive decision to join the SS, largely a response to students who chided him about being too ideological (an ardent anti-Bolshevik and strong believer in pan-Europeanism), and for not turning his beliefs into action.

In the end, I found Voss very credible. He seemed to struggle earnestly, openly, and in great detail. He wasn't shaping a story to exonerate himself as many Nazis did, but to understand himself. Voss seemed to be peeling his own onion well before Grass.

Expanded Visions

The notion of a "thoroughly decent" SS officer led to this chapter's diversion. It caused me to seek a story that might loosen my stereotypes of SS soldiers as holding unshakeable beliefs in the full Nazi ideology and particularly its antisemitic core, and as being doggedly unrepentant after the war. Before stating where I landed in this search, I want to acknowledge that I am sticking my toes into the particularly vast, deep, and turbulent waters of Nazi Germany and the Holocaust, and that I am very much an amateur in this arena.

But a great value of my quest to find my uncle is that it enticed me, here and there, to reflect on things I haven't thought much about, notably family silences, heroism, and my stereotype of Waffen-SS soldiers. After publication of this book, I'll likely expand those reflections, but I've wanted to share them here because they were an important part of my journey and because they might encourage some readers to reflect on the topics themselves. My neophyte reflections, however, are just that. They are not pronouncements and certainly not made with the insights, for example, that a grief counselor might bring to the question of silence, or that a war hero might bring to the question of heroism, or that a scholar, perpetrator, or victim of the Holocaust might bring to the questions raised in this chapter.

That understood, the clearest insight I gained had to do with after-war responses and it was not a big surprise. Many SS soldiers, including almost all individuals convicted at Nuremberg, remained immutably committed to the Nazi cause and unrepentant after the war. Voss is quite a contrast to this—introspective, regretful, seeking to understand his own illusions. And he is even more nuanced, for example, struggling to reconcile his deep regret with his continuing love of Germany. Intransigence and shamelessness on one hand, and introspection and regret on the other form a continuum. I don't know where along it most SS soldiers fell. Perhaps experts have studied it and know. But my bits of information provided little sense of where Wolf Zoepf fell. Voss felt that Zoepf had changed, though he provided no specifics. An Alsatian couple we'll meet shortly found Zoepf to be arrogant, and they focused on an action that suggested that, perhaps, he had not changed very much after the war.

Here are insights that arose as I explored the other feature of my stereotype, whether being in the SS required unquestioned commitment to the full Nazi ideology including its dominant and engrained antisemitism. In essence, I found that my stereotype probably fit well in 1940 when Zoepf enlisted, but not so tightly in 1943 when Voss enlisted. In 1940 acceptance into the SS depended not only on voicing a commitment to the Nazi ideology but also on demonstrating that commitment. For many, proof probably consisted of their high achievement in Hitler Youth groups. But most would have come to that full commitment naturally, as products of the pervasive culture of deeply engrained antisemitism that had existed in Germany and most of its territories for a long time.

This was the case, for example, in Zoepf's Latvia. Although its sizable Jewish population had been granted important civil rights and were at least tolerated early in the twentieth century, that changed after a coup in 1934. Under Karlis Ulmanis, Latvia became a dictatorship and Jews became an increasing, though unofficial, target of repression. A letter of May 27, 1940, from US Envoy John Wiley in Riga to Secretary of State Cordell Hull summarized this situation, albeit in modulated language.[100] It began:

> I have the honor [a prescribed State Department phrase]
> to report that anti-Semitism [*sic*] appears to have been
> adopted as the policy of the Latvian Government. No official

pronouncement . . . has been made and . . . such a policy is
denied. . . . In Latvia as elsewhere there has probably always
been some anti-Semitism. Before 1914 there appears to have
been good and mutually beneficial relations between the
dominant German Baltic class and the Jewish commercial
and professional community. The Latvians and the Jewish
minority seem on the whole to have lived together in
relative harmony. The full vigor of the present anti-Semitic
drive seems to date only, curiously enough, from the recent
"repatriation" of the Baltic German minority.

It would have been highly exceptional had Zoepf's beliefs varied
greatly from those of this general culture of antisemitism.

Of course Voss grew up in a nearly identical German culture. He
too would have been exceptional if he had evaded the strong influence
of engrained antisemitism. But he offers a story that suggests that, by
virtue of family influences, he was an exception. I found his story
plausible; others might not. But I wondered whether he could have
held this belief and been accepted into the Waffen-SS.

When Voss enlisted in 1943, the SS was in a very different
situation than in 1940. By then it and the Wehrmacht were
becoming desperate to find soldiers, and the SS had begun to
relax its traditional, rigid requirements. A US military intelligence
report from that year stated that "less attention is being paid (by
the Waffen-SS) to the political and racial qualifications of recruits"
and gave instances in which "Nazi ideology is no longer regarded
as an indispensable qualification." It concluded that "the original
conception of 'SS-Tauglichkeit' (Aryan ancestry and National-
Socialist beliefs) has been abandoned."[101]

So by 1943, the SS would readily have accepted a person such
as Voss—a seventeen year old with a solid Hitler youth resumé—
regardless of whether he joined on impulse or adhered to the full
ideological commitment. Perhaps no one even inquired, for by then,
as George Stein who studied the Waffen-SS extensively suggests,
traditional criteria had not only loosened but unraveled. Stein notes
that "the largest group of western volunteers joined the SS for such

non-idealistic reasons as a desire for adventure, status, glory, or material benefit."[102]

In a word, it seems implausible to imagine Zoepf enlisting without a full commitment to the party line, but more plausible to imagine Voss joining with a much more selective commitment that notably didn't include virulent antisemitism. Of course, there is a powerful bottom line to all of this: belief for SS soldiers was almost inevitably tested by orders to commit atrocities. This was the basis of the blanket condemnation of all SS members by the Nuremberg Court. Voss, however, claimed that he and his buddies committed no such atrocities. An article from the Jewish Virtual Library gives credence to this possibility. It recognizes that there may have been a few SS units that were exceptions, such as those assigned to the sparsely populated Russian-Finnish border where there were few if any Jews. It specifically states that "divisions like the Nordland and Nord have virtually spotless records."[103] The "Nord" is the 6th SS Mountain Division Nord to which both Zoepf and Voss belonged.

An astute friend noted that the failure to commit atrocities was a matter of circumstance, for had these troops been assigned to commit atrocities, they would have done so. As a lawyer, I'm wary of condemning people on the grounds that "they would have if they could have." But even if it is a dangerous legal test, it is a profound moral test. I'm sure Voss was plagued by this test, and I suspect most if not all SS soldiers would fail it. If ordered to commit atrocities, they would have. But I also suspect that this would have been the case for many German civilians. And I suspect it might even have been the case with some officers on the *Dunera* heading to Operation Dragoon, and for numbers of American soldiers and civilians back home whose antisemitism, had circumstances placed them in Germany in the 1930s and '40s, might well have led them to join in Holocaust atrocities. Actually, this thought introduces my final bit of reflection.

Impelled by the reference to a "thoroughly decent" SS officer, I set off on this tangent to find a story, presumably his, that would loosen my vision of SS soldiers as one-dimensional, automaton-like, immoral, faceless, unrepenting Nazi antisemites. I didn't find a helpful Zoepf story, but I found a helpful Voss story. Through it, I could begin to imagine more nuanced human beings beneath my simple stereotype. Some people might worry that such stories give escape routes to those who want to deny responsibility and that they encourage efforts at revisionist history (currently rampant in various places in Europe) in which nations, cultures, and peoples try to distance themselves from their histories of deep antisemitism and downplay their complicity in the Holocaust.

That certainly isn't my intent. I believe it is vital to insist on full responsibility for the atrocities of the Holocaust and to come to grips with the profound reality of engrained antisemitism. It is equally vital to see nuanced human faces beneath our stereotypes lest we fail to recognize how susceptible we all are to cultural demons and dynamics like those that fomented the Holocaust, and that continue to cause and threaten genocides of various marginal groups around the world.

Giving Meaning

15

Louis

I worked too hard

In that morning instant of January 7, 1945, on that frigid ridge in the Vosges Mountains outside of Wingen-sur-Moder, France, Phil's life and the meaning he could give to it ended. All that remained was the meaning that survivors might now confer.

The amorphous public automatically bestowed its generic meaning: a war *hero* who had made *the ultimate sacrifice*. But within that public were some who knew Phil well, as a son, brother, husband, or close friend. Quite in contrast to the general public, they each faced a very personal grief. They also had very personal memories to draw on as they struggled to give meaning to Phil's life and death.

Earlier I characterized my family's response to Phil's death as silence, but that is only how *my* generation experienced the response. Obviously for Louis, Bessie, and others close to Phil, silence was merely a façade that usually hid their overwhelming grief and kept memory after memory bottled up within.

My older sister Gail vividly recalls spending a day at our grandparents' home when she was eight or nine years old (perhaps in 1948–50). Late in the afternoon she was sitting at the kitchen table where Grandpa Louis ate his cornflakes at 4:00 a.m. every morning and was watching Grandma Bessie stir a pot on the stove. Suddenly Grandma burst into tears. Dropping her spoon in the pot, she fled toward the dining room into the arms of Grandpa who joined her with loud, choking wails.

Our Uncle Herm who was also present came quickly into the

room, bundled Gail into the car, and drove her home. No explanation followed, so we don't know what caused the outburst, but it is easy to imagine that it was set off by some random thought about Phil. Even if Phil wasn't the source of this particular outburst, he must have been the source of many similar ones by both Bessie and Louis.

I wanted to learn more about the grief experienced by Phil's inner circle, about their memories, about the ways that each tried to make sense of his life and death. Of course, I was many years too late for this, but I was able to get a glimpse of several of these things, and I'll share what I found. They begin with Grandpa Louis.

Americans assessing the life of Phil's father Louis would likely see him as a modest American success story. They would note his humble beginnings in Russia, his immigration, his hard work peddling fruits and vegetables by cart, and ultimately the founding and operating of his profitable wholesale grocery business, Levy-Ward. I'm sure this accomplishment made Louis proud, but it was not what he felt was the crowning achievement of his life. That achievement was bringing his family out of Europe, out of the Pale of Settlement, to America.

Most certainly, he would have given anything to have his boy back alive, but since that wasn't an option, Louis, age sixty-five when Phil was killed, turned his attention to restoring his most cherished accomplishment. "I spent too much hard work bringing my family out of Europe to leave my boy there," he announced as he set about the task of bringing Phil's body home.

The desire to bring dead soldiers back home has a long history. For example, Thucydides reported on the custom as it was practiced in 431 BC in Athens:

> Three days before the ceremony, the bones of the dead [killed in the Peloponnesian War] are laid out in a tent which has been erected; and their friends bring to their relatives such offerings as they please. In the funeral procession cypress coffins are borne in carts, one for each tribe; the bones of the deceased being placed in the coffin of their tribe. Among these is carried one empty bier decked for the missing, that is, for those whose bodies could not be recovered.[104]

In the United States, for the past two centuries, our military has provided a way for at least some families to have the remains of their sons or daughters returned. Early efforts were informal and limited by a lack of resources and other complications. In the Civil War, at least a few dead soldiers were returned to their homes as new retrieval, identification, and return policies were developed.[105] Then, with World War II, Congress adopted a sweeping new policy, a universal commitment to return retrieved bodies if a soldier's family desired it.

Of course centuries ago, when warriors fought within a few hundred miles of home and killed one another one at a time with a club or arrow or spear, the process of retrieving the dead and bringing them or "their bones" home was relatively simple. But when 405,000 boys die thousands of miles away across oceans and continents, often in masses at the hands of bombs and machine guns and artillery fire and grenades, the process is much more complex. Bodies need to be retrieved, identified, transported, provisionally buried or somehow preserved, and later exhumed, transported, and reburied.

Michael Sledge has written extensively about this subject, detailing the complex process of retrieving, identifying, and returning the remains of "soldier dead," a term once used to refer to the collective dead rather than any individual soldier. Finding bodies years after they have fallen or been left in unmarked graves is difficult. Retrieval can be dangerous as it is, for example, during battle or in areas with land mines. The forensic work of identifying a body or perhaps a decayed body or only a body part is often very complicated. Dog tags, if decipherable, have simplified this process as has DNA testing, but prior to these aids or in situations where they aren't helpful, the identification of a body can be arduous and involve examining evidence such as clothing and personal items. Further complications can arise in exhuming or transporting bodies.

The soldiers who do this work and the military as a whole are committed to care and accuracy. In part, they are fulfilling a soldier's deep commitment to bring back his buddies, and on a larger scale, they are helping families face the death. Sledge puts it this way:

But there does seem to be a universal theme that reverberates through the centuries; humans want to see their dead, if at all possible. Only then is the passing of a loved one real. Only then can we say our good-byes and begin to form a new social consciousness for those who have [died].[106]

Acceptance of the death allows the family to move beyond death to shape a new identity for their loved one:

By finding the mortal remains of those who have died in military service, we recognize their sacrifices and thereby keep them from becoming unpersons. . . . They are our warriors, and they represent, on a national level, our belief system. On a personal level, they represent the willingness of individuals to support, protect, and even die for the values, ideals, and security of our nation-state. By bringing their remains home, we help bereaved families form a new social identity for them; by recognizing their contributions in our cemeteries and ceremonies, we attempt to give their sacrifice meaning.[107]

The return and interment of a soldier is a familiar, ritualized drama. The casket and its burial symbolize the reality and finality of death. The flag surrounding the casket symbolizes the soldier's new social identity—*hero*; and a well-decorated officer handing that flag to the family invites them to accept this new identity. The ritual seeks to transform a corpse into a hero and, modified a bit for un-retrieved bodies such as sailors lost at sea or for those remaining in cemeteries abroad, this ritual was repeated hundreds of thousands of times after World War II.

Tell Me About My Boy . . . the Quartermaster's 1946 pamphlet written for families, described the new Congressional policy and the process adopted to implement it.[108] It briefly described the complexity of retrieval and return of remains, including factors such as climate, transportation availability, and the speed of production of items needed for this work, probably as an alert to families that the process could be very slow. Then it identified the four options that families would have: Remains could be buried in a permanent United States military cemetery overseas, returned to the United States for private burial, returned for burial in a national military cemetery in the United States, or returned for burial to another nation.

The right to choose was initially offered to a spouse if the soldier was married and the spouse had not remarried. Next in line were the soldier's adult children, if any, then the soldier's father, and finally the soldier's mother. Holders of the right to choose could waive their right in which case the right transferred to the next in line. Families were notified of this process, but they could not exercise their choice until the military was ready to exhume and transfer the body. Because the work was slow and because foreign cemeteries were being "evacuated" in a designated order, a family might have to wait some time for the return of the body.

All costs of exhumation, preparation of the remains, casketing, and forwarding to the designated place were borne by the government. The government paid $50 toward the cost of a private burial, but remaining costs and all arrangements were to be made by the family. Burials all included a casket wrapped in the American flag and the delivery of that flag to the family by a military officer at the end of the service.

The military explained that "every possible step has been taken" in their work so "there is absolutely no question of the positive identification of the remains." Pieces of evidence used in this process such as dog tags, clothing, or personal items were placed in a casket at the time of the provisional burial and, upon exhuming, were rechecked to verify the identity. Then, to assure that there would be no confusion or tampering with a body, the body was "guarded by military escort" until its reception by the next of kin.

The pamphlet gave the clear impression that fulfilling the Congressional mandate would be a massive, arduous, costly endeavor—and slow. In fact, Phil's remains would not get to South Bend until December 1949, almost five years after he was killed! To Louis, who was nearing the end of his own life, five years must have seemed like an eternity. After all, it had only taken him five years to migrate to America and then bring over his entire family.

Initially I wondered if there had been complications that delayed the "repatriation." One possibility was that bodies are not disinterred as a general rule in Judaism, and both the Hebrew Orthodox Cemetery in South Bend and Phil's father would have been very sensitive to that rule. But the rule has multiple exceptions including several that would have applied to Phil; for example, the original burial was only provisional, so the burial in South Bend was actually a burial rather than a disinterment and reburial; sons could be moved to lie with their parents; Jews buried in a non-Jewish cemetery could be moved to a Jewish cemetery. I don't think questions of religious doctrine delayed the process.

Another potential complication seemed more likely. I read an account of the recovery, identification, and return for burial of Second Lieutenant William J. Sheard. He was among those who crossed the German border on the same date as Phil—December 15, 1944—and was killed in Bundenthal, Germany. The account identified serious complications in retrieving, identifying, and moving Sheard's body that seemed to delay his return to Holyoke, Massachusetts, until August 15, 1949.[109] Since Phil died and was returned about the same time as Sheard, I imagined that Phil's situation had created special identification complications similar to those with Sheard. Knowing what I knew of Phil's death—the grenade, a bazooka perhaps, and a fire—I imagined that making a definitive identification was difficult and could have been the cause of the delay.

But eventually I learned that the process was slow for everyone. Beyond the work necessary to find and deal with remains, permanent cemeteries had to be planned and built to replace temporary ones. And there were many American Military Cemeteries, about fifty in Europe. Temporary cemeteries followed the troops and were expected to be reasonably close to the front lines so that body collection centers would not be far from burial points. So, for example, the cemetery at Épinal, France, was the initial cemetery used by American divisions of the Sixth Army Group fighting in the Vosges. Since advancement was slow on each of the three fronts in the Vosges for some time, Épinal served well; but when troops in the northern Vosges pressed forward, added cemeteries had to be created, namely one at Niederbron, near Strasbourg and another at Hochfelden. Cemetery use was in flux at the moment Phil was killed, so I don't know where his remains were temporarily laid to rest. In all, the remains of 280,000 soldiers were handled in Europe out of approximately 310,000 soldiers killed or missing there. Of these, 170,000 were returned to the United States after temporary European burial. Another 100,000 soldiers were killed or missing in the Pacific Theater including many whose remains were returned home. So, the sheer scope of the foreign preparation of remains resulted in an understandably slow process.

Preparations on the home front also took time. Fifteen distribution centers for receiving remains and transferring them to families across the country were designed and built, procedures were developed for distributing bodies, and personnel were hired and trained for the work. For example:

> One of the unique features of distribution center operations
> was the use of uniformed escorts of the same branch of
> service and in the same or higher grade as the deceased. The
> escorts accompanied each remains from the distribution
> point to the final destination. This practice involved direct
> and personal contact with grieving relatives and required
> carefully selected young men, endowed with proper tact,
> courtesy, and sympathy. The duties . . . were drawn up in
> [standard operating procedures and in] detail before the first
> deceased reached American ports. . . . Each escort would
> receive all necessary verbal instructions, be briefed . . . on
> the importance of their mission, and be required to witness
> the motion picture "Your Proudest Duty" before going on
> a mission. Upon arrival at their destination, escorts were
> expected to help and comfort the bereaved in every possible
> manner, including attendance at the funeral if this was
> requested. In each case, the escort was directed to remove
> the American flag from the casket and present it to the
> next of kin. Upon completion of each mission, he would
> return immediately to the distribution center and report any
> unusual occurrences. . . . [110]

The first "repatriated" bodies did not reach the United States until the fall of 1947—from the Pacific Theater on October 10, 1947, in San Francisco, and from Europe in New York City on October 26, 1947. Much of the distribution occurred within a year or so, and by the time Phil's body arrived, all distribution centers had been closed except for San Francisco and New York City. By December 12, 1951, all centers were closed. The cost of handling 280,000 bodies— ones that remained in Europe and repatriated ones—was about $160 million or $564.50 per remains. At the peak periods in 1947, there were 13,311 employees involved in this effort overseas and 2,149 in the United States.[111]

By the time Phil's family was provided with the four choices, Barbara had remarried (in October 1946), so the choice fell to Louis. He, together with Bessie, chose to bring Phil home for burial, and I would guess that Nathan handled communications with the army.

Phil's casket was returned to the Hay Funeral Home in South Bend, and Phil was buried in the Hebrew Orthodox Cemetery on December 16, 1949, the day after his mother's sixty-second birthday. It was a clear but cold and blustery day according to weather reports, and Phil was buried in a plot next to those reserved for his parents. His mother would come to occupy her plot within two years (Bessie died November 9, 1951), and his father would join them in two more years (Louis died December 15, 1953). I imagine that, true to tradition, an officer presented the flag to my grandparents. I wonder if there was a small or large group of mourners to throw their shovelful of dirt on the casket in the Jewish tradition. I very much wonder if Barbara was there.

Louis's prime life achievement was again as intact as it could ever be. He and Bessie had their boy back home.

16

Nathan

A short trip to eternity

Nathan was thirty-five years old when his younger brother was killed. By then, he had joined a prominent South Bend law firm after struggling as a solo practitioner and, at one point, seriously considering a career in radio. He and Norma had been married for eight years and had built a new house on LaSalle Street in 1941, the year that Norma quit her job at the welfare department and gave birth to Gail. I arrived in 1943.

By January 1945, Nate and Norma also were beginning to pursue their common humanitarian passions in ways that would punctuate their lives. They were creating an extremely diverse circle of close friends that crossed race, class, religion, and education lines, and they saw these friends frequently. They were becoming involved in community justice work and soon each would be a significant leader in South Bend. Among various activities over the next three decades, Norma would serve on boards of directors and help modernize programs of the local orphanage, promote the African-American settlement house (Hering House), help found the Women's Council on Human Relations, start a chapter of the Urban League and serve a term as its president, establish a collaborative family planning service in heavily Catholic South Bend, and plan and often lead many activities of the local Conference of Christians and Jews. Nathan would preside over the board of the local United Way and promote several innovative projects within it, chair the National Budget Committee of United Way, serve as president of South Bend's Anti-

Poverty Program, lead an investigation into local jail conditions, and arbitrate labor disputes, having gained the trust of both management and labor.

By 1945, Nathan and Norma were about to introduce Gail and me to social justice. Soon they would teach us friendship songs and we would all sing together around the piano—"I'm proud to be me, but I also see, you're just as proud to be you"; "You can get good milk from a brown-skinned cow, the color of the skin doesn't matter no how"; "Close your eyes and point your finger, on the map don't let it linger, any place you point your finger to—there's someone with the same type blood as you." A few years after this, at our nightly dinners, they would involve us in discussions about social issues and their community activities. Not long after, they would begin to include us in visits with their friends, in events such as the ecumenical Seders they began to hold at our home in the 1950s long before such Seders became more popular publicly, and in special occasions such as meeting Nina Agarwala and Florence Adadavo, exchange students at St. Mary's College who soon became family friends.

It was certainly no happenstance that Gail and I each shaped careers in social justice work and that we each became lawyer/social workers, following in the footsteps of our social worker mom and our lawyer dad. Nor was it happenstance that our efforts were devoted to bringing people together across lines of difference and promoting inclusion of people at the margins of our society. We inherited our parents' deep commitment to "bridging."

By the time I was thirty-two years old, both Nathan and Norma had died, so I was denied the types of conversations with parents that tend to occur when children are older, have lived more life, and are more settled and accomplished. When Gail and I talk about this, we wonder, for example, how consciously Mom and Dad shaped their extraordinarily diverse group of friends or what they saw as their biggest challenges to raising us. Among the many, many conversations I would love to have with them now are discussions about Phil. Most specifically, as I neared the end of my research, I wanted to know how Nathan handled Phil's death and framed a meaning for his life and death.

Of course that conversation was impossible, so I reluctantly accepted the two clues I had. One large clue was my dad's silence. Throughout my life I took this to mean that Phil's death, and even his life, were too painful for Dad to talk about. The other small clue I had was the advice that Nathan apparently gave to Mark Van Aken, Phil's best college friend, in a letter notifying Mark of Phil's death. Mark refers to this advice in his condolence letter back to Nathan:

> Just seven days ago I received two letters, one from you and one from Barbara, each telling me that Phil died on January 7th. You must know only too well how this makes me feel. . . .
> You expressed the thought . . . that Phil would not want us to mourn for him long. You are right . . . but I might add that this is easier said than done. I find that my rational powers are not always in control of my emotions. I can't reason or rationalize away such sorrow as this. . . .

Nathan often hid strong negative feelings behind his robust rationality, and I assumed he was doing this here. I'm sure for him as well, "moving on" would have been much "easier said than done," so advising it helped cover his own inability to share and handle his grief.

I had nearly completed my research and the first full draft of this book when Gail and I got together for one of our frequent visits. She carried a plastic storage box that contained some items from the several boxes of family memorabilia we inherited. For the most part, we hadn't looked at these items for the forty years since our parents died. There were several pictures of Phil, of Phil and Barb, and of our parents and grandparents. One was a picture of "Lee Douglas" speaking into a WSBT Radio microphone. Gail had found an envelope with a baby picture, birth announcement, and letter from Mark and Dolores Van Aken letting Mom and Dad know of the birth of their new baby (ultimately their only child) named Phillip. "Just thought you might like to see a picture of Phil's namesake," they wrote. There also was a December 1936 letter from a law school professor who had heard that Dad was struggling to establish a law practice and was considering a career in radio instead: "I want to write and say don't. I still feel, as I have always felt, that you are a born lawyer and in my opinion the most likely eventually to succeed of any man in your class." I thought as I read this, had any of my own professors recalled that struggling student at the back of the lecture hall and offered advice to me, it would have been to grab one of those good radio offers as fast as I could.

Gail pulled a final item from the box. I recognized it immediately as one of the two unpublished books our dad had written. I hadn't looked at them for a long time and only remembered that they both dealt with discrimination, one a novel that I had and this work of non-fiction that Gail kept. This book, apparently submitted to some publisher and rejected, was in a brown binder with its typed, carbon-copy pages held on the left by a clasp. The jacket said:

PRIDE IN PREJUDICE

OR

BUILDERS IN BABEL

Submitted by: Nathan Levy

The book had no date, but two references to "recent" events—the atomic bomb test on Bikini Atoll and the murder of four "Negroes" in Georgia—enabled me to date the book to 1946 or 1947.

I began to leaf through the book's 258 pages beginning with its lengthy table of contents. Each of its sixty chapter titles adopted the format of the book's title. For example an early chapter is entitled, "Meeting the Problems, The Words and The Author or Here's a How-de-do." ("Here's a Howdy Do" was one of Dad's favorite songs from Gilbert and Sullivan's *The Mikado*.) Another chapter is entitled, "The Rule of Anger or This Has Happened Before," while another is, "Some More About the Risks of Discussion or Can You Recognize Arrogance?"

The chapter titles reflect seriousness amidst playfulness, and the book's preface explains this more directly. It says that this book is "about people and the trouble they have getting along with other people in groups." It warns that eventually "we shall speak of the death of millions of people" but also promises humor and playfulness "because it is too much of a burden to make of a book a funeral." Nathan surmises that, "Although I was not present in the concentration camps, I am willing to believe that there were jokes in the face of death."

I turned to the first chapter, "The Kind Of Thing That Goes On or A Short Trip To Eternity," and read its first sentences:

> It is not far from Italy to France. Even by water it is not far. But when the trip is for purposes of invasion, the sense of anticipation adds years to hours.

I was stunned—as shocked by these sentences as I had been to read Wolf Zoepf's reference to the flickering light of the tank burning behind him. Rather than "silence" or "moving on," my father had written a book in Phil's memory!

I wouldn't have recognized this when I perused the book almost forty years earlier after my father died and before Gail and I packed his keepsakes away, for Phil is not mentioned by name in Chapter One or anywhere else in the book. He is only revealed here and there by allusions, such as this one to his trip from Naples in Operation Dragoon, so I could only recognize Dad's book as one about his brother after doing *my* Phil research. I continued reading. The next paragraph contains essentially the only direct characterizations I have of Phil:

> The minutes passed slowly as bad days pass. In the semi-darkness below deck were American, British, and French officers desperately striving for calmness, each feeling he'd succeeded in hiding the effects of the mental strain so obvious in the others. Among these was a young American of six feet, of twenty-two years, of a new, fresh, philosophical nature. Included in the arts which he practiced was a keen, native-like knowledge of the French language. He had

practiced the language and accumulated this knowledge because of his love for French thought and literature, a love later heightened by the pain which he felt in the destruction of the body politic of France, the starving of its children, the chaining of its spirit. This pain was deep, personal, sincere. On a growing mind of considerable power, World War II made a mark that led the young American to feel invasion and battle were for him not alone an opportunity to serve his own country and people, but were blows struck to free France, the people of France, the mind, the soul of the French people.

Suddenly the scene changes.

In the semi-darkness the voices could be plainly heard, the liquid French, the broad English, the many kinds of American. In the French, then, and suddenly, harsh, mean, violent words of attack upon the Jews of the world. The young American stiffened. Is this France? Are these the French? Is this the spirit and the thought of the people I love? Did I study my French, did I learn my French and come here to be able to understand these words?

All things pass it is said. And pass they did—the conversation and the hours and the hell of invasion and battle.

Far, far from the Mediterranean shores of France, north through the Valley of the Rhône, and beyond the Vosges to a place small and cold in the land of France went this young American who was, by creed, a Jew; who was, by choice, in the front lines; a young, eager, idealistic, somewhat bewildered boy, an American and a Jew. America has lost him, and he loved and believed in America. France has lost him and he loved France. People, mankind, have lost him to whom people were noble and good, to whom mankind was worthy.

I never knew my eloquent father to be more eloquent, but I also never heard him angrier than in the chapter's final paragraph:

The French officers drink their wine, smile upon their
women, recall the hours before invasion, and recall the
invasion and victory with honor and glory sufficient
to themselves. Not even in the semi-darkness of their
consciences is this boy who died to protect their wine, their
women and their recollections recalled.

How did my father deal with this heavy burden of anger? I
didn't have to wonder long because, by Chapter Two, the anger had
disappeared and the book had become a treatise on intolerance. The
book is vintage Nathan, filled with big, profound ideas and wonderful
insights; built step-by-logical-step by a skilled analyst and veteran
debater; making very serious points with humor and captivating
stories, and sometimes being a bit abstruse as, for example, when
he turns the process of finding the cubed root of a number into a
metaphor for something. For me it offered a wholly unexpected
answer to my question about how Nathan responded to his brother's
death, an equally unexpected social justice conversation with my dad
almost forty years after he died, and an equally unexpected current
reminder of my playful father with a big brain and a big heart.

Essentially the book offers this line of thinking: Intolerance by
groups—especially people grouped into nations, religions, and races
or ethnicities—is at the heart of the great evils of the world, its
discriminations and segregations as well as its wars, slaveries, and
genocides. This intolerance is built on pride or arrogance, the notion
that one's nation or religion or race is superior to others (smarter,
stronger, more truthful, more humane, etc.). Add power to one such
group and its treatment of the others can turn to abuse that ranges
from gauche to ghastly.

Tolerance—accepting others—is certainly preferable to intolerance,
but it retains the seeds of intolerance. It allows groups to hold onto
their separate identities and feelings of superiority even as they restrain
themselves. Almost inevitably at some point, restraint wanes and
powerful tolerant groups revert to intolerance. This poses the central
human relations challenge of the world: How might people get beyond

tolerance and attain some deeper sense of appreciation (respect, love) for one another?

Nathan offers no major answers, recognizing that answers will likely take generations to evolve. He urges caring people (he calls them "liberals") to get on with the task of imagining such answers and offers one idea. He notes that much humanitarian work in the world is organized around the very categories—race, religion, nationality—that are at the heart of intolerance, and offers a list of examples, including: American Relief for China, the American Jewish Joint Distribution Committee, the United Yugoslav Relief Fund, the many American aid and advocacy efforts aimed at "Negroes," and self-help groups of Catholic Veterans, Polish Veterans, and Hungarian Veterans. He admits that he supports and participates in numbers of these efforts, but offers an alternative. Suppose aid was based solely on need and that hunger organizations, for example, offered to help any starving applicants, not just hungry Czechs or hungry Frenchmen. Nathan is trying to imagine human services that eliminate the types of distinctions that nourish pride and prejudice.

I mentioned earlier that the book is vintage Nathan in various ways. It leans into controversy, for example. At one point in investigating *power*, it identifies uncomfortable similarities between "intolerant tough boys" like Hitler's contingent, and "tolerant tough boys" like the judges at Nuremberg. At another point, he acknowledges his strong support of the United Nations that was just forming but criticizes its Security Council, which grants special veto powers to seven nations. By granting these nations special rights based on their great power and sense of superiority, the UN, he argues, has retained and institutionalized the dangerous seeds of intolerance.

It also is vintage Nathan in its use of stories and its playful way of presenting serious ideas. Early in the book, Nathan tells this story to illustrate that readers already know some things about intolerance. One day at some crossroads in Germany during the war, a black American MP "expertly" keeps military vehicles moving through. Along the road there are "little people down in the ditches . . . all authors or victims of the horrors of torture, war, starvation and destruction." During a break in traffic, these people scramble out of the ditch and continue their travels. A displaced Pole flees east pushing a wheelbarrow with his belongings and a displaced Czech goes in the same direction; a displaced German goes west with his wagon, a displaced Frenchman goes south, and a displaced Jew goes north. Suddenly a crisis erupts. The Pole's wheelbarrow tips and a chair drops on the Czech's leg. He falls into the path of the German whose wagon overturns as it runs over the Czech. The wagon's contents fall onto the Frenchman who . . . falls into the Jew who . . . falls into the MP. The story adopts the classic disaster-leading-to-disaster plot of "this is the house that Jack built."

Then Nathan gives readers a test, and predicts that all, no doubt, will get perfect scores. He asks: "Which participants made the following remarks?"

1 God damn Pole
2 God damn Czech
3 God damn German
4 God damn Frenchman
5 God damn Jew
6 God damn Nigger

Nathan built this story, I suspect, from Phil's story about his fellow soldiers helping the Italian with a cart.

In another example of gravity and humor, Nathan tells this true story: "Among my good friends is a couple. . . . The husband is a displaced Kentucky hillbilly; the wife a displaced Mexican girl." Gail and I knew this couple and their children well. "Their daughter, Anne, is about the same age as the daughter of a Jewish family we (Norma and I) know and we heard that the Jewish girl had mocked Anne, calling her 'half-Mexican,' and Anne had responded by tossing her head high and replying, 'You're just like everybody else. I'm different.'"

> The next portion of this little story takes place some
> weeks later when my wife, a good, estimable woman, who
> was sticking her nose into other people's business at the

time, happened to meet the little Jewish girl, and said, "I understand that you go to school with Anne. We know Anne (and her family). It must be lots of fun to play with her." The little Jewish girl was unmoved by these rapturous words. She shook her head [and said] . . . with some vehemence, "My mommy doesn't like Mexicans."

Nathan is having fun with words, fun telling a story, fun poking a little fun—and at the same time illustrating one powerful way that prides and prejudices are passed on.

At the end of his book, Nathan returns to World War II and recalls the great Allied landing at Normandy. For several pages he describes the massive brain power and creativity required to carry this off—to plan the landing, amass and train a million men, manufacture and transport the equipment, produce and gather the supplies, and so forth. "And there on the beaches of Normandy landed the men, the machines, the guns, the shells, the thousands and thousands of items. . . . An achievement . . . greatly admired . . . as an unparalleled example of the organizing ability and genius of men."

> Think of how much greater would have been the
> achievement of the brains that were used, think of how much
> larger and impressive would the concepts have been that
> would have made it possible to land no one on the shores
> of Normandy, to build no machines of death, to create no
> bombs, no shells.

No doubt, as Nathan wrote these words, reverberating through his heart and mind were the words of a soldier left unnamed who once sat aboard a ship on his way to battle and, on pages 30 and 31 of a journal he was keeping, scribbled:

> I become sick inside when I think of my beloved America
> squeezed dry of her resources in order to make thousands
> of ships, planes, guns, tanks, uniforms (of cloth that should
> have made cute little dresses for pretty little girls) . . . of the
> men killed and maimed. . . .

Can we apply as much force, energy, foresight, to winning the Peace?

People will sacrifice to kill the Jap or German, but will they fight Ignorance and Poverty with equal energy. . . . We have the physical power necessary. We have resources. We have ideas. Will we locate the driving force for the greatest undertaking ever contemplated by the human mind?

Nathan and Norma with Gail and the author, about 1947 when Nathan was writing *Pride in Prejudice*

17

Mark

There's one more thing

My Aunt Jean, Phil's youngest sister (now deceased), turned eighty-five in 2011. The birthday turned into a small reunion of the few of us remaining on the Louis Levy branch. I had begun my research on Phil and shared some of my findings with the gathering, including a picture from "The Package" of Jean with a handsome young boy who looked a bit like Elvis. "Who's that handsome guy you're with?" I asked her. "Oh, that's Mark Van Aken," our aunt replied. Gail and I hadn't heard this name for many years but recognized it immediately as Phil's best friend at college. "So that's Mark Van Aken!" we exclaimed and then asked, "Is he still alive?" Aunt Jean wasn't sure. The last she heard he was a professor at the University of California.

When I got home I found a phone number and address for him, and a reference identifying him some years before as a professor at UC Hayward in the Latin American history department and as the author of a few books on Latin America. Before trying his house, I talked to a former colleague of his at UC who told me that Mark had retired twenty years earlier but still attended faculty meetings occasionally. He let me know very politely that Mark's memory wasn't what it used to be but added that Mark's wife, Dolores, was very sharp and might prove helpful.

I called Mark on March 20, 2011. Dolores answered the phone. I introduced myself and we spoke for a while. She and Mark met well after Phil had died, but she knew immediately who I was. After all,

Mark Van Aken and Jean

as she let me know, their only child was named Phillip. She put down the phone and went to speak with Mark. In a moment or two, Mark got on the phone. He was obviously delighted by the call. "Always good to hear the name 'Levy.' Of course I remember Phil. He was my best friend in college." Mark began to recollect those old times. Originally he and Phil met in their dorm ("What was the name of that dorm, darn it?"). Phil was a year ahead of him and Phil roomed with his "second [best] friend, and I was his first friend." He and Phil loved to talk together. Mark loved to dance and went to sorority and fraternity houses and clubs where Phil's band was playing.

It became clear, as I asked some follow-up questions, that Mark didn't remember very many details from those days and had forgotten some very major things as well. For example, he didn't remember that he had ever met Phil's wife, Barbara, or his sister, Jean, or my parents. I knew otherwise but didn't say so, and I shifted to matters he might have an easier time recalling than ones that had been fading without many prompts for seventy years. He was born in Elkhart, Indiana, but moved to Coldwater, Michigan, early in his life and that's where he grew up. His father had a floral shop in Elkhart and then worked at a greenhouse in Coldwater. Mark had gone to Michigan and been in ROTC (he didn't recall that Phil also had been in ROTC) and had graduated from Michigan before entering the navy where he served with an anti-submarine unit in the Philippines. Upon returning from the war, he got a PhD in history from the University of California at Berkeley, focusing on Latin America. He lived and taught in Argentina for a time while he was completing his PhD and then joined the history faculty at Hayward. He and Dolores were married several years later. Mark repeated what Dolores had said, that their only child was a son, Phillip, and added emphatically that Phillip was named for my uncle and knew this well.

I asked Mark about the books he had written on Latin America. He couldn't recall the names of them but left me on hold for a couple of minutes and returned with the books in hand. Slowly he read me their titles and told me a little about them. All focused on the liberation of Latin American nations. I told him that I had been in Nicaragua twice and had learned some things about its history and that of Latin America, and that I wish I could have had a course with him. He told me "that was far in the past."

I returned to questions about my uncle. "What did Phil major in?" Mark wasn't sure, but figured it was history because that is what Mark had majored in. "Had Phil been in the debate club?" Mark wasn't sure but figured that he probably had been because Mark had joined the debate club probably with the encouragement of Phil. I asked what Phil might have been had he returned from the war. Without hesitation, Mark said, "a college professor." Clearly Mark could only imagine a Phil who had taken the same directions that Mark would follow.

Suddenly, Mark recalled the name of the dorm where he and Phil lived—Lloyd Hall in the West Quadrangle. But for the most part, he had few specific recollections from those olden days. At a point, there seemed to be nothing left to talk about, so I was about to thank him for his information and end the conversation when Mark said, "There's one more thing I want to tell you." Then, as close to verbatim as my rapid scribbles could manage, he said this, in very measured words:

> I grew up in a small Michigan town. My father had a college education at Michigan State University but not a very good one. He was rather insensitive and often made prejudiced remarks about Jews. [Dolores said something in the background and then Mark added:] But my mother wasn't that way.
>
> Meeting Phil and his friends was about the first contact I had with Jews, and I learned how prejudiced an atmosphere I had been brought up in. Phil and I often spoke about the war and about the Nazi treatment of Jews. It left a deep impression on me. Phil was the major influence in my re-education.

To further emphasize the depth of Phil's influence, Mark told me that he had a twin brother John who had died just a few months earlier. John had also gone to Michigan, but hadn't become a friend of Phil's. In contrast to Mark's embrace of new ideas, John had retained the less open viewpoints of their father.

Soon after talking with Mark and writing these notes from my conversation, I reread Mark's letter of condolence to my father after my father had notified him of Phil's death. Mark was surprised at my father's composure. He quoted my father as saying that Phil wouldn't want us to mourn him long, "but," Mark responded, "that is easier said than done."

Then he added this entry. Filled with cliché, it could easily be dismissed as sweet sentiments aimed simply to comfort both the sender and recipient—had it not been so prophetic:

> But I do find some comfort in remembering Phil for the swell guy that he was. It's a strange thing too that in a way I don't have to *remember* Phil; he became so much a part of my life that I need only to feel conscious of him rather than remember him. I believe that anyone who knew Phil well can understand what I mean.

So, as I told Barbara, in a sense we can say that Phil has
not died for he lives on in the hearts of those who loved him,
as a son, as a husband, as a brother, as a friend.
   The seeds of his life have taken root in us. We must
cultivate them and make them thrive.

Phil, indeed, had taken root in Mark. Even sixty-six years later,
when specific memories of Phil had become lost in the fog, Mark
could clearly recall for me the Phil who had been embedded within
him for life. Mark had truly cultivated those seeds—an open mind, a
heart that could seek and embrace diversity, a concern for liberation
and social justice—and they had become his moral compass in life
and the source of so much meaning and fulfillment for him.
   There's one additional way that Mark figured prominently in
my search. Certainly being the first to cross into Germany was the
highlight of Phil's military career, but I wondered about another
accomplishment. He wanted to be a First Lieutenant. At the time of
the crossing, he still was a Second Lieutenant, saying in his January
2 letter home how embarrassed he was that the *Stars and Stripes*
called him a First Lieutenant. So I wondered if he perhaps had been
promoted posthumously or perhaps before he could be informed of
the promotion. Then I reread a condolence letter of February 3, 1945,
to my Aunt Jean from Mark Van Aken:

> Dear Jeannie,
>   Today I received the letter from you which I hoped never
> to receive. . . .
>   I do have some news for you which won't help any but
> which you may like to know. Three days ago I received a
> letter from Phil dated January 2nd and postmarked Jan. 6th.
> He was in very good spirits at the time and wrote me a swell
> letter—as usual. He mentioned that he had received notice of
> his promotion to 1st Lt.

Phil must have been promoted to First Lieutenant on January 2,
sometime after he wrote home and before he wrote to Mark.

18

Return to Petit Wingen

It is my duty

We leave Colmar, home of Auguste Bartholdi, designer of the Statue of Liberty, and drive north through France's Rhine River Valley toward Petit Wingen. The Vosges Mountains form an imposing western border to the valley, their green-forested slopes just beginning to show streaks of red and yellow on this warm mid-September day in 2014.

Every few miles the forest opens narrowly to reveal a small medieval village punctuated by its ancient defenses against harm—a gray ruin of a castle on a cliff above the town, and a sparkling steeple reaching from the town square toward heaven. Actually most towns here have two spires, one Protestant and one Catholic. They reflect the mixed heritage of the Alsace region, perpetually crisscrossed by armies and alternately flying the French and German flags. Seventy years earlier, these towns needed an added line of defense and received it.

Phil is on our minds as my wife Elizabeth, my sister Gail, and I wend our way toward Wingen. He would have been thrilled to travel leisurely through this autumn landscape, but his visit here seventy years earlier was quite different. The trees were bare, the air was frigid, and he surveyed the scene from the turret or through the commander's scope of his Sherman tank, "Chick."

As his unit slowly advanced, liberating many Alsatian villages, Phil would have noted the church spires; but in some villages he also would have noted the Rue Des Juifs—"Street of Jews"—and noted that no Jews joined the liberation celebrations. Writing home he said,

The Rue des Juifs in Bouxwiller, an Alsace village near Wingen-sur-Moder

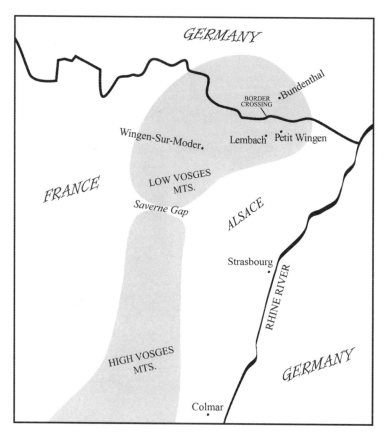

Area in France visited in 2014

"I'm afraid to ask, 'Where are the Jews?'" In Alsace the answer would have been that most had been transported to Auschwitz.

We drive across the Saverne Gap that divides the High Vosges from the Low Vosges, which continue north just into Germany. When Phil and the Allies cut through this gap, the French units continued east to liberate their beloved city of Strasbourg while the American forces turned north into the Low Vosges and continued, as we were doing, toward the French-German border. Earlier we described the "first across" border crossing by Chick and its crew on December 15. They had just liberated Petit Wingen that morning and the nearby town of Lembach the day before. The unit log of the 191st describes the Lembach liberation:

(December 14): Company "C", supporting 180th Inf Regt, made decisive gains in their assault up the main road leading through the Valley to Lembach and Wingen. Attacking from 031434 [a position], the first platoon supported the swift advance, culminating in the taking of Lembach. On the route toward Wingen, the platoon took numerous prisoners. Upon their entrance into town, the lead tank [not Chick] was hit by enemy tank fire—this enemy tank was fired on immediately and knocked out by No. 5 tank of the platoon. The tanks assisted the infantry in the clearing of the town. . . .

We are due for lunch at 12:30 p.m. at a restaurant in Lembach. We arrive a bit early. Soon a woman and two men dressed in hiking boots, jeans, and work shirts arrive and walk toward us. I reach out a hand to Eric Schell, Sean Schulze, and Sean's wife Elisabeth, and we all make introductions and take seats in the restaurant. Shortly after, Jean Weisbecker, the mayor of Petit Wingen, joins us. Conversation is lively but complicated by our multiple languages. The mayor speaks French and German; Eric, French and English; Sean, German and English; Sean's wife, all of these languages; and my family, only English and smatterings of French and German. Taking time for translation as we go, we all tell each other a little about ourselves.

Eric is from Alsace, works at a bank, and is about forty-five years old. His parents experienced the war as children. His father survived the fighting in Strasbourg. His mother, age five at the time, lived under Nazi rule and then survived the devastating battle of Hatten-Rittershoffen by living for five weeks in a cellar with little food and water. Hatten was essentially leveled when she and her family emerged. For years, Eric has studied the war, particularly battles in Alsace, and has honored Americans who fought and died here. He has helped visiting Americans, helped identify bones found, and participated in ceremonies at the American Cemetery in Épinal, France, where most Americans killed in Alsace are buried.

Sean is American, a career army officer in the US Army, and

Luncheon with, left to right: Gail, Mayor Jean Weisbecker, the author,
Eric Schell, Sean Schulze, Elisabeth Schulze

stationed in Germany. He is about fifty, and his wife was born and
raised in Bavaria. Like Eric, Sean has an interest in the battles in
Alsace. The day after our lunch, he and Eric are going to Épinal to
honor Cecil Harris, a private from Kentucky, whose bones were
recently found and identified.

Mayor Weisbecker appears to be in his mid-fifties. He teaches and
has been mayor of Petit Wingen and its 475 inhabitants since 1983.
The town has roots in Roman times and an identity that reaches back
to the Middle Ages. The mayor grew up in town and his parents lost
their home in a battle there.

During dessert, I tell the gathering a little about our uncle. I tell
them that we grew up not knowing much about him and that I decided
in retirement to try to learn more. I say that I discovered a great deal
about him, much to my surprise at this late date—that I knew of
his school involvements in music, debate, and student government,

and his romance with Barbara; that I found a few old friends who remembered him well; that I learned about his military career from battalion logs, letters home, and a wonderful journal he kept while heading to Operation Dragoon. Sean and Eric seem to take great care interpreting my words for the mayor.

Eric mentions that he has always wondered why Americans fought in France to preserve it for Frenchmen, so I end my remarks by explaining that Phil seemed to have three reasons for fighting. He loved America as did his immigrant parents and was eager to serve his country. He loved France, was distressed by its loss of liberty, and was anxious to help liberate it. And he was Jewish, alarmed at what was happening to the Jews of Europe, and impatient to intercede. Well before Pearl Harbor, he decided to be a soldier. Then I present each of our guests with a copy of the initial "Family Edition" of my book and we go outside to commence the journey that has brought us together. In a four-car caravan led by the mayor, we drive up a rutted, one-lane dirt road to the French-German border.

Earlier I mentioned the Internet network that encompasses the 191st Tank Battalion. In the spring of 2012, Mike Poole from the network posted the 1944 *Stars and Stripes* article about the first Allies across the border. Sean happened to see it and was intrigued by its mention of soldiers carving their names in border stones when making notable border crossings. He contacted the network's point person, Dave Kerr, who provided him with the latitude and longitude of the crossing point and possible names of men in the 191st Tank Battalion and 45th Infantry Division who likely were among the troops who crossed the border on December 15. Sean contacted his friend Eric, and the two hiked the border in search of the stone carvings in May 2012.

Along the border, which is in a remote, mountainous, and wooded area, they found several stones with markings, including the one they were taking us to see. Phil had carved his name in a stone and, incredibly, Sean and Eric found it. So far this is the only stone that can reliably be linked to the crossing of Phil's unit.

We pull our four cars off to the side of the road, and Eric and

Border stone with letters unaltered

Border stone with letters highlighted with carbon

Sean lead us to the spot about one hundred yards away that they had discovered on their hike. At this point, the national border is simply a small, dry streambed, certainly nothing like the mighty Rhine that forms the border on the east of France. They lead us to border stone Number 26. Like the other stones, it is a rectangular pillar, perhaps eight inches wide by five inches deep and three feet high. A straight sightline is painted white on its rounded top, pointing the way to the next border stone.

The author with his sister Gail (right) and his wife Elizabeth at the border stone

The others stand back respectfully as Elizabeth, Gail, and I inspect the stone. From Sean and Eric's picture, we know what to expect. Still, it is chilling to see the stone's original date, 1826, and chiseled under it, "Phil P" and the date "12/17/44." *"Here's your Uncle Phil,"* Sean and Eric had originally written when they sent me the picture.

There is some doubt about the etching, however. The date—two days after the crossing date of December 15—poses no problem. There was no time to stop and chisel a name as the units fought forward on the fifteenth, but much more time to return once they had established their base in Bobenthal, Germany, a mile away. But the

Examining the border stone

name itself casts some doubt—we wonder why Phil would sign his name, "Phil P" rather than "Phil L" or just "Phil" or perhaps "Phillip."

I can't explain this but feel confident this was Uncle Phil because I have checked lists of others who might have crossed that day and have not found other "Phils" or soldiers with a last name such as "Philpot" or "Phillips" that begins with "P-h-i-l." But my sister is a retired judge and needs more proof. She kneels in the mud next to the stone and examines it closely. "PHIL" is carved squarely and fairly deeply with notches that suggest that letters were chipped. The second "P" and the date are less deep and scrawled as if scratched rather than chipped. Then, next to the second "P" Gail sees and feels another "H" and perhaps a very vague "I" and a more definite "L." The second "P" seems to begin a separate attempt to carve "PHIL," a less effective etching, perhaps a first attempt. Our camera doesn't pick up the scratches but Sean confirms them.

At least we have a new theory for what we want very much to believe without reservation, and are more fully convinced that this was the work of *our* Phil. Of course, even if there is some doubt about the engraver, there is no doubt about the "first across" accomplishment thanks to the *Stars and Stripes* article.

It took us seventy years to find Phil, and we have come to know and love him very much, so it isn't easy to leave the border. We don't want to leave the site of the high point of his military career or to abandon him to his fate.

The mayor invites us back to his office where he presents us with a beautiful book of the history of Wingen and a copy of a DVD from the town archives. We thank the mayor profusely for his gifts and for taking such time with us. He knows only a little English, but it is enough to understand our thanks and enough to shape a response. "It is my duty," he says and shakes our hands.

When we get home, we view the DVD. It contains some amazing film footage of the war by the Signal Corps and several interviews with local survivors. One film clip entitled *Wingen* shows infantry men moving through town and is dated December 15, 1944, the day of the border crossing. In it, for a few brief seconds, a tank approaches the camera and quickly passes by. Two men stand in its turret, faces indistinct in the old film but not too blurred to leave us wondering. After all, there weren't many tanks in Petit Wingen that day. Several weeks later we visit Jack Del Monte, Phil's old tank mate, and show him the film. He is amazed and very moved by the film, but he notes that there is a gun mounted on the front of the tank and tells us that none of the tanks in Phil's platoon had such a gun. Another film clip is dated January 6 and seems to take place in the other Wingen, Wingen-sur-Moder, where Phil was killed on January 7. That clip ends with several men removing a soldier, probably still alive, from a tank to a stretcher. It is not Phil's tank but the vivid image is all too chillingly similar to what would happen again the next day.

A January 2015 letter from Mayor Weisbecker shares additional information with us. It adds that this spring he will have a chance to speak of us and of Phil when Wingen and Lembach celebrate the seventieth anniversary of the end of World War II.

19

Return to Wingen-sur-Moder

I am a soldier

We have a second appointment, this one in Wingen-sur-Moder, the other Alsatian town called "Wingen," lying thirty miles west of Petit Wingen. Three miles short of our destination, we check into our hotel in Wimmenau. Wimmenau is where the 191st Tank Battalion established their provisional headquarters for the defense against Operation North Wind, and it is where Phil and his platoon came on the night of January 3 when summoned back to France from Bobenthal, Germany. It was also where Jack Del Monte saw Chick, parked in front of headquarters three days after Phil was killed, apparently towed there to be restored or salvaged.

In the morning we drive toward Wingen. Almost immediately we come to the junction with the D-12 Road where, on January 4, Phil turned north toward the ridge just hours after Wolf Zoepf and his men had come down from the ridge to attack the town. Our original plan was to follow Phil's route up the D-12, but those plans had changed several days earlier. In a last-minute Google search, I discovered that Wingen had a small museum devoted to World War II. The reference provided no contact information, but stated that the museum was in the home of a couple named Bergmann. I e-mailed Eric Schell to see if he knew the couple. He had heard of them but didn't know them.

Perhaps a half hour later, I got an e-mail from Linda Bergmann. Eric had discovered a way to reach her, had explained our situation to her and provided our e-mail address, and she had contacted us immediately:

At the Bergmann home: left to right, Jacky, the author, Linda

A member of my association sent me a Mail. We can help you to find the position in the woods where your uncle was killed during January 45. My husband know the place were the tank was knocked out.

We know the story and spoke with the German who was there at that time in the woods near the Kohlhutte.

Linda apologized for her English, and in my excited response to her, I let her know her English was just fine and we would love to meet them. She e-mailed back:

Tomorrow at 5 PM I will have a reunion in the City hall. If you want to com at 2 PM would be perfect.

Thursday will also be perfect. I will show you my small Museum and my husband will go with you to the position in the woods.

What a miraculous last-minute discovery! We decided not to visit the ridge until we had met the Bergmanns.

As we drive into town, I expect to recognize various sites from the battle, but I recognize only two. On a hill to our right is the Catholic church where the Germans imprisoned the two hundred soldiers they captured in their surprise attack on January 4. Also on our right are the railroad track and the underpass on the east side of town where Zoepf and his men initially gathered for their escape the night of January 6. In the distance to our right, the ridge looms above the town.

We find the Bergmanns' address and park in a short driveway next to their motorcycle repair and ambulance business. A woman in her mid-fifties with blond hair and a big smile comes out to greet us and introduces herself as "Linda." We hand her flowers we have brought and she leads us inside, through the shop where we briefly meet Jacky, and into a building behind their home. The museum is simply a corner of a large room and it contains a number of pictures and other artifacts and memorabilia on shelves. Linda shows us some of these items and then we sit around her wooden table.

Our conversation is primarily with Linda, for Jacky is working in the repair shop. After some brief small talk, Linda begins to tell us about herself and Jacky and their work. Jacky is from Wingen-sur-Moder and she is from Sarre-Union, twenty miles away. They dated in school, she got pregnant, and they got married. Jacky was Protestant and she was Catholic, German Catholic. "Now, I'm only Catholic when I'm sad," Linda adds. Jacky grew up in their current home although it's been considerably changed. During the Battle of Wingen, his mother fled town as did most others, and when she returned, she found three German bodies on the first floor and on the stairway. Linda specially mentions that Jacky's best friend was Jewish and in their wedding party, and that Jacky was in his as well.

Linda's parents owned a restaurant, and they lived behind the Rue Des Juifs where Linda played with Jewish kids. On the Sabbath when Jews are prohibited from doing chores such as turning on lights, Linda would go to their homes and do those chores for them. This was the 1970s, I believe. After the war, some Jews who had survived the Holocaust moved back to Alsace, and the area also experienced a surprisingly large influx of other Jews, many from Africa.

At home and school, in Alsace with its strong German ancestry, Linda and Jacky learned almost nothing about Hitler, Nazis, the war, or the Holocaust. At some point, Jacky read a book about these things and began to "hate Germans." Linda also got interested, and they learned a great deal about these topics including local Wingen war history. For years now, both have become war buffs with a strong commitment to honoring the American soldiers who liberated France.

Jacky—Linda describes him as "a realist" in contrast to herself, "emotional and a dreamer"—studies battles and collects artifacts of the war including ammunition and equipment that still can be found now and then in and around Wingen. Both of them have helped many visiting American veterans and their families learn about the Battle of Wingen, and Linda names several particularly close American friends including one whom they visited in the United States. At least annually, they make a pilgrimage to Normandy where Linda feels she can speak to the soldiers on Omaha Beach. Recently, she asked them for a sign to acknowledge her faithful presence. Looking down, she discovered an old rusted rations can floating in the shallow water—proof, she beams, of her mystical connection with "my boys."

Linda is particularly energetic as well as passionate. Single-handedly, she made the local arrangements for two joint reunions of American and German veterans of the Battle of Wingen. At these events, she got to know Wolf Zoepf as well as Johann Voss. Since she got no help from town government, she had to finance these efforts through donations from businesses, a brochure that she created and sold, and a considerable amount of her own savings. She arranged for a plaque to be installed near the church in 1991: "In Tribute to the Men of the American 174th and 176th Infantry Divisions Who Won the Freedom of Wingen-sur-Moder, 3–7 January 1945 and in Memory of Those Who Gave Their Lives in This Battle." A piece of this memorial had recently broken and Linda was arranging for its

Plaque honoring the American Veterans of the Battle of Wingen-sur-Moder

repair. An e-mail she sent after we returned home proudly included a picture of the repaired plaque.

Trailblazer, the newsletter of the 70th Infantry Division, reported on the memorial dedication and concurrent reunion. Stating that Linda had "arranged for the municipality to give the wall on which are the sculpture and plaques," it referred to her as "the guiding spirit for the occasion" and noted that the numerous Blazers whom she has befriended over the years are "unanimous in their praise for her initiative, dedication, and hard work" in establishing the museum and the memorial.[112]

Linda tells us that the 101st Airborne Division made her an honorary Screaming Eagle, and proudly shows us her certificate. The 101st Airborne served in the Battle of the Bulge and in Alsace, and went on to capture Hitler's hideaway in Bavaria near the end of the war. A decade later, then-President Eisenhower assigned the Division to escort and protect students who were integrating Little Rock High School.[113]

Our talk with Linda is wide-ranging and detailed—family history, current family situations, help provided to American families, friends they have made, ongoing commemoration of the Allies. But she glides past our questions about Wolf Zoepf and his relationship with them. After an hour and a half she invites us to return the next day, and Jacky takes us to the ridge. On our way he takes us through town and points out various locations such as Zoepf's headquarters, the Red Cross infirmary, the underpass, and the headquarters of Allied commander, Wallace Cheves, in Villa Frantz on a western hill. Then we drive to the D-12 and turn north.

My heart is pounding as I try to place the findings that are so familiar to me on paper into the surrounding landscape. *There, on my left—that must be the long, steeply sloping field that Zoepf and his exhausted men struggled across through the snow in the early morning hours of January 7. Here is where they must have joined the D-12 and continued their march. This must be about where they paused to regroup at the hotel, but where is the hotel? Apparently it disappeared long ago. The Forest Road must be just ahead—yes.*

We turn right onto that road and immediately come to a small parking area. We stop, get out of the car, and begin to walk that last several hundred yards that Zoepf and his men walked. Actually, in the late 1990s, Jacky accompanied an aging Wolf Zoepf to this exact spot. Zoepf was unable to walk down the road more than a few hundred feet, but he was writing his book and wanted to check his recollection of the location to confirm his story and to ensure that his maps were correct.

The forest is isolated and dark, still covered by a thick canopy of leaves even on this late fall day. But we notice little around us as we walk, eyes forward, down the narrow dirt road. We round the curve that the Germans rounded just a few hundred yards from where they would squeeze by a snow-covered American tank in the dim, early hours of January 7, 1945. Then, we are about where the tank stood.

We are speechless, trying to comprehend the moment; but we remain only a brief minute or two, for Jacky seems anxious to move on. He points out the vague remains of foxholes on the flat land on the right and large rocks to the left that still have visible scratches

Curve on the Forest Road: left to right, Gail, the author, Jacky

Location of Phil's tank on the Forest Road

where bullets ricocheted. Jacky leads us to the end of the road and points to the location across a ravine where the Germans had taken their position after being pushed off the ridge the day before Phil was killed. Jacky needs to be back home, so all too soon we return to town, thank the Bergmanns for the day, and confirm the time we will meet them tomorrow.

Then, Gail, Elizabeth, and I return to the ridge. We need more time and privacy to take in the moment. We try to imagine what the road looked like in that winter of 1944–45 with its heavy snowfall; what it felt like in that year's record cold. We look at the trees around, thinking that they were silent observers of that scene seventy years earlier until we realize that few if any of them existed that long ago. We look more closely at a foxhole, at some bullet marks on rocks. We try to imagine a hulking Sherman tank blocking the road and a line of exhausted soldiers edging by it. Gail and I think about the uncle who barely knew us and whom we didn't know at all. Suddenly an old man pushing an older wooden wheelbarrow filled with firewood passes by and nods. We nod back. He must wonder what brings visitors to this lonely place.

Emotions explode in all directions. Regret, as my quest comes to an end, collides with gratification at its successful completion. Wishing my family could be here undercuts my sense of fulfilling a duty to them—to Barbara and Phil, to Louis and Bessie, to Nate and Norma. The visit seems alternately a funeral and a rebirth. Overall, however, the moment feels profoundly sad.

∾

There is a story I have hesitated to tell you. Earlier I mentioned the network of veterans of the 191st and others with an interest in the battalion. Denis Berger who was with the 191st is a point person for the network. He and Merle Stevens used to organize reunions of the battalion and Merle also published a newsletter. When Merle died, Denis inherited Merle's substantial cache of materials and added it to his own. In 2012, I called Denis, a very energetic ninety year old, and shared my story about Phil, Wolf Zoepf, and the grenade outside Wingen. He said that for some reason it sounded familiar and promised to dig through his boxes to see what he could find, warning that this would take awhile because he was in the process of moving and his boxes were in great disarray. Two days later I got an excited call from Denis. He happened to find some correspondence dated 1996 from a member of the 180th Infantry Division, and it seemed to involve my incident.

When Wolf Zoepf was preparing his book, he posted a request in the *45th Infantry Division News* asking if anyone had further information about the tank incident on January 7. John Russell of Wisconsin, in the infantry unit to which Phil's tank was attached, had been an eyewitness to the event, and shared his vivid memories with Zoepf. He also sent copies of their correspondence to Denis who now shared them with me. Here is the recollection Russell shared with Zoepf:

> Before dawn of January 7, your [Zoepf's] unit attacked as was expected. [All other information I have shows that the "attack" was unexpected.] You knocked out our tank and set it on fire. This was a major blow to our defense, but it turned out to be a blessing. The fire illuminated the top of that hill and silhouetted every individual movement of your troops. We could see you, but you could not see us in our fox holes. It was like a shooting range with targets all over. . . .[114]

"A blessing"? Only the hideous distortions of war—the momentary rescue of Zoepf's men, the shooting range lit up for Americans—could find some blessing on that road on that day. But today there is a blessing as we stand where Phil died. Silently my sister says Kaddish (the Jewish prayer for the dead) and gathers some pebbles from the road to place, next time we are there, on our family gravestones in South Bend—Grandma, Grandpa, Mom, Dad, Phil.

The next day we return to the Bergmanns. This time, Linda invites us to sit in their cozy dining room. She seems more relaxed. Jacky has more time to join us. She pulls out files and boxes of correspondence that line one wall. When we renew our efforts to learn more about Wolf

Zoepf, she is responsive and begins with this story about him. When Zoepf took over Wingen on January 4, 1945, he set up headquarters in a vacant house but soon felt that the neighboring house would be a better location. He and an aide visited and found a family there. Most Wingen inhabitants had fled, but this family stayed to tend to a sick grandmother. Zoepf ordered them out, and when they explained they had to stay, he told them, "You'll be sorry," and left. The aide, a few steps behind him, warned the family in a whisper, "He means it." Were the two playing good cop/bad cop? Perhaps, but the family took no chances. They were gone when Zoepf returned to take over their home.

In his book, Zoepf also refers to this incident, naming the Mathié family. He mentions that they moved out of the house he was commandeering, but makes no reference to coercion being involved.[115] He also describes an incident occurring on January 6 when he and the German command are hunkered in a basement somewhere and they take in three old people who were burned out of their home by Allied artillery fire.[116] The portrait of Wolf Zoepf continues to be incomplete and imprecise.

Searching through her files, Linda selects a 1991 Christmas letter from Ruth Zoepf, Wolf's wife. She and Wolf had visited Riga, Latvia, twice that year, the second time to join in celebrating the recent Latvian independence from Russia "commemorating the long struggle against Bolshevism," and in the letter Ruth opines that three hundred thousand Russian soldiers still occupy the country so "the real work only starts now." Linda gives us copies of this letter and a reunion brochure from 1989.

The letter reminds us that Zoepf's Latvian origins and Baltic German identity were fundamental to his view of himself and his family, providing a possible window into his impulse to join with the Nazis against the Russians. The possibility fits with this observation from an article in the Jewish Virtual Library: "While it is difficult now to understand why anyone would volunteer for the Waffen-SS, during the war the organization was presented as a multinational force protecting Europe from the evils of Communism."[117]

Something seems to have loosened the reticence we experienced yesterday whenever we asked about Zoepf. Perhaps it is simply our persistence in asking questions or perhaps Linda and Jacky have come to believe that we are sincere and trustworthy listeners who will value their conclusions. In any case, it soon becomes clear that the Bergmanns did not like Wolf Zoepf very much. They recall the formality with which he and his Mountain Division veterans introduced themselves at the reunions in Wingen-sur-Moder. They would stand erect, snap their name, rank, hometown, and end with a click of the heels. I was advised later that traditional salutes were commonly banned in post-war denazification processes, so those in attendance would have recognized this as an act of defiance. Quite in contrast, the Americans casually introduced themselves by telling about their families and careers. The couple was particularly bothered by the following remark by Zoepf in an address he gave to the assembled French and American soldiers: "You should be proud that you were able to fight against as elite a unit as mine." Jacky and Linda sum up their opinion of Zoepf in a few sharp words— "an actor, arrogant, still a Nazi sixty years later." [They would later clarify that they meant "Nazi" in pride and demeanor, not beliefs.]

By contrast, their friendship with Johann Voss, the author of *Black Edelweiss*, was a warm one. They knew Voss by his real name rather than the pseudonym under which he published his book— and they found him to be quite "genuine," a real person and not an "actor."

Somewhere in that final conversation, Linda says, "The women in this town, they. . . ." She makes the hand movements of knitting. "Knit," we say. "*Voilà*," she says. "They knit and they play tennis. I—" Her voice deepens with gusto and a touch of levity. "I am a soldier." And she certainly is. She has picked and fought her battles well.

Our visit ends with hugs. The journey is over.

Several chapters ago I told you of discovering that the introduction to an unpublished book by my dad talked about Phil's death without naming him. Angrily—more so than I ever heard him—my father berated Frenchmen for what he anticipated would be their future failure to acknowledge the sacrifice of American soldiers generally and Phil in particular.

> Not even in the semi-darkness of their consciences is this boy who died to protect their wine, their women and their recollections recalled.

Dad would have been thrilled that Frenchmen like Linda, Jacky, Eric, and Mayor Weisbecker have dedicated large parts of their lives to honoring those Americans who, like Phil, came across the sea to defend and liberate France, even their tiny villages nestled in the Vosges. Dad would have loved to see the genuine and reverent welcome these people gave us as representatives of our Levy clan. And he would have been ecstatic to have been wrong in his prediction that Phil would be forgotten by the people he helped liberate. At least for this dedicated handful of Alsatians, that is emphatically not the case.

Epilogue

Stories and Silences

Stories are capricious. Some create silences; others break them. Some stories are myths that vilify, spreading stereotypes that "justify" genocide, slavery, exploitation, invasion, and discrimination. Others are myths that glorify, hiding lives under cascades of ticker tape, perhaps, or some other whitewash of heroism. Yet other stories are simply scared away by the profound grief of one generation that cannot share them with the next generation who, as a result, never hear them. In each case, the stories of millions of people are eradicated—stories of the joys and sorrows, achievements and failures, and the myriad adventures that marked their various passages across this lonely planet.

But some stories can break silences. In fact, they may be indispensable to that task. They may interrupt stereotypes and rise above them, turn dins to songs or even symphonies, flow into voids. Some stories may appear in the mail in the form of a journal, long buried in a widow's bureau, exhumed at her death. Some may surface from the bottom of a cardboard box of family memorabilia in the form of an anonymous introduction to an unpublished book. Others may be etched on a stone, found by hikers, deep in the woods along the French-German border. Yet others may be recollections of a ninety-year-old veteran with a razor sharp memory, shared sixty-seven years after a war—"Sure I remember Phil—and wasn't his wife's name Barbara?"—who then digs out a letter he sent home to his mother on December 8, 1945, that she kept and he still keeps close at hand:

As you probably noticed my platoon leader is Lt. Levy
without a doubt the swellest guy I've run across in the
army—he's from South Bend, Ind. (he doesn't read our
letters—that's why I said this).

The world today is deluged with life stories and fragments,
confessions and self-advertisements, eagerly published, Facebook-
ed, tweeted . . . spun, guarded, puffed, and promoted. Perhaps our
great Babel of words would be much better off if we could exchange
some of these for life stories wrapped in our family silences.

~

After Phil died, my family went forward with their lives. His siblings
and their spouses finished school, entered marriages, raised kids,
and advanced their careers. Barbara remarried, began a family, and
practiced social work. Phil's parents moved forward albeit more
slowly with fewer demands in their lives and only a few years left
to them. My vague childhood recollections of my grandparents (I
was eight when Grandma died and ten when Grandpa died) are that
they were old and usually somber, but there were bits of liveliness.
Grandma Levy, with a twinkle in her eye, would give my buddy Tom
and me a penny to taste-test the cookies she had just baked. Grandpa
loved baseball and attended most games of the South Bend Blue Sox,
a team in the women's professional baseball league that flourished
while the boys were away and for a few years after. But mostly I
picture my grandparents as weary and sad, and I tend to attribute
much of this to Phil's death.

Now, as a parent, I can imagine that their grief was complicated
by guilt. They were devoted parents who understood that their first
duty was to keep their children out of harm's way. And my father also
felt guilt beyond his grief, perhaps seeing himself as the protective,
older brother who had failed in his job; perhaps feeling that, as the
eldest son, he should have fulfilled the family's civic duty and enlisted,

fought, and sacrificed his life. At any rate, after Phil died, Dad decided to enlist but was talked out of it by his family.

My family didn't adopt the personal identity of "hero" for Phil— no shrine on the mantel with his picture or a flag or his Purple Heart. But my family was also unable to shape any other personal identity for Phil. Most sadly, they weren't able to find a way to celebrate his good life, his accomplishments, and even his promise. I'm sure they each recalled many good things, frequently at first and then more sporadically, but they kept these memories to themselves, fearful that sharing them would unleash waves of their own suppressed grief or unleash that sort of grief in each other.

So the family identity for Phil, which might have been a volume of lively stories, was silence instead.

Imperceptibly, my generation inherited this silence. For the few of us who sit on the branch below Phil on our family tree, the silence was there and Phil wasn't. We hadn't lost him; we simply never had him and rarely had reason to wonder about him. If we wondered a bit when we visited Louis's and Bessie's graves and his adjacent headstone or whenever Barbara visited South Bend, we chose to maintain the silence, for it was easy to sense the great pain Phil's death had visited on our family. We were drawn into the silence and perpetuated the void that it assured.

Practically speaking, we were just youngsters and rarely interested in family history. Then pretty soon we were young adults and too busy shaping our own identities to think about uncovering hidden identities from the past. And then we were mature adults with full lives that lacked the leisure needed to explore family history. Anyway, by then most of those in the generations ahead of us had died and left more immediate empty spaces in our lives.

Here's a story that suggests the place of Phil throughout most of my life. Many decades ago, I found a bugle of Phil's at home in South Bend. My musically talented uncle apparently had learned to play it and probably played reveille and taps somewhere for his army training or service units. At the time, other than a few books, the bugle was the only possession of Phil's that I had, but it didn't at all pique my interest in learning more about him or his musical abilities. Nor did I value the bugle as a sacred heirloom. It stood alone, an interesting artifact, without a context.

In the metalwork portion of my junior high Shop course, we all had to fashion a hammerhead for ourselves. I enthusiastically worked on my hammerhead, grinding and polishing it, but after hours of work, it turned out to be considerably lopsided, which surely contributed to the "C" I got in Shop that term. Now, with the bugle, I had this idea of turning it into a lamp—cord up through the mouthpiece and pipes, bulb in what apparently is called the "bell" of the trumpet. I moved forward on this project with the same old enthusiasm that I had applied to my hammerhead. Unfortunately, my work proceeded with the same poor level of craftsmanship, for the bugle soon had no resemblance to either a trumpet or a lamp. Not long after, I threw its remains away.

Here's a story you know. In the late 1970s, my wife and I had dinner with Barbara and her husband, Gil. Obviously it would have been inappropriate to discuss Phil there, but I met with Barbara alone after that. I could have asked about Phil but I didn't. It probably didn't occur to me, but if it did, I was programmed too deeply not to break the silence with what I imagined would be uncomfortable questions. In retrospect, I realize that talking with me about Phil might have been a great comfort to Barbara even if somewhat painful for her. Of course, Barbara didn't raise the topic of Phil with me either. I imagine that she, too, was accustomed to the silence. Only in death could she break that silence by having Phil's journal sent to me.

That package was finally able to wake me in a way that the bugle had not, and this book is my effort to break the silence and fill the void. It offers a bit of biography as a more fitting individual identity for Phil than *public hero* and a more deserving family identity than *silence*.

Obviously I'm too late to break the silence for Phil's immediate family, too late to offer a "new identity" to them, and too late to

Phil's journal

build a more complete biographic identity that pulls from their considerable recollections. In fact, I'm barely in time to offer this thin vision of Phil to my own aging generation; and if the legacies of most of us essentially fade from view about two generations after we die, my work is just in time to disappear in favor of a simple name and date stuck on a branch above me on our family tree.

❧

But at least for a brief moment our family silence will be filled by this story, a shovelful of life tossed into the void.

Notes

1. Alan A. Michie, *Retreat to Victory* (Chicago, New York: Alliance Book Corporation, 1942).

2. Armiger (Joe) H. Somers, "Memories from Another Century," in *Notre Dame Magazine*, Spring 2004.

3. For a picture of the contest victor, Louis Bellson, with H. H. Slingerlands, see: Gene Krupa Photo Gallery.

4. Arthur J. Hope, "Chapter XXVI," in *The Story of Notre Dame* (Notre Dame, IN: University of Notre Dame Press, 1999).

5. John Mellencamp, "In Performance at the White House: A Celebration of Music from the Civil Rights Movement," February 9, 2010.

6. Timothy White, "John Cougar Mellencamp; Rebel With a Cause," *The New York Times Magazine*, September 27, 1987.

7. Jewish Virtual Library, s.v. "Russia."

8. Indiana Department of Natural Resources, St. Joseph County Jewish History.

9. Garnet (Rose) Lutes, "Paying for his Lodging," "A Footsore Traveler," "Two Days of Rest," "Friends From the Old Country" in *Mishawaka Enterprise*, April 2, 9, 16, and 23, 1970, Mishawaka, Indiana.

10. See, for example: Karen Brodkin Sacks, *How Jews Became White Folks and What that Says about Race in America* (Rutgers, NJ: Rutgers University Press, 1998); Eric L. Goldstein, *The Price of Whiteness: Jews, Race and American Identity* (Princeton, NJ: Princeton University Press, 2006).

11. Egbert Ray Nichols, ed., *Intercollegiate Debates* (Yearbook), Volume XXII (New York: Noble & Noble Publishers, 1941), v.

12. Egbert Ray Nichols, ed., *Intercollegiate Debates* (Yearbook), Volume XXI (New York: Noble & Noble Publishers, 1940), 35.

13. Rafael Medoff, "Kristallnacht and the World's Response" (Jerusalem, ISR: Aish HaTora, reprint, 2003).

14. Adolf Hitler, "Speech to the Reichstag on the Jewish Question" (January 30, 1939).

15. Laurel Leff, *Buried by the Times* (New York: Cambridge University Press, 2006).

16. Deborah Dash Moore, *GI Jews: How World War II Changed a Generation* (Cambridge, MA: Harvard University Press, 2004).

17. "History," The Official Website of Fort Knox, Kentucky.

18. Sports Illustrated, "Pat on the Back," in *Sports Illustrated*, February 6, 1956.

19. "Skin Diving Record For Women Set," *The Wilmington News*, January 19, 1956 (Wilmington, North Carolina).

20. Adams Burns, "The Pennsylvania Railroad's "Southwind," American-Rails website, www.american-rails.com.

21. Moore, *GI Jews*, 198.

22. Ibid., 169–70.

23. David McKittrick, "Walter Foster: Champion of Anglo-Austrian Friendship," *The Independent*, December 31, 2009.

24. National Geographic TV, "Churchill's German Army, Biographies: Willy Field."

25. See, for example: Mario Cacciottolo, "The Dunera Boys—70 Years On After Notorious Voyage," BBC News, July 10, 2010; Alan Parkinson, "From Marple to Hay and Back," (The Marple Website, n.d.); *Wikipedia*, s.v. "HMT *Dunera*."

26. Michael Danby, "Danby talks to the Dunera Boys," *J-Wire* (Jewish online news from Australia, New Zealand and Worldwide), November 19, 2009.

27. Michael Blakeney, *Australia and the Jewish Refugees, 1933–1948* (Sydney, Australia: Croom Helm, 1985).

28. Winston Churchill, "Wars Are Not Won By Evacuation" (June 4, 1940, House of Commons), in *Never Give In: The Best of Winston Churchill's Speeches*, ed. Winston S. Churchill, the prime minister's grandson (New York: Random House, 2003), 217.

29. Danby, "Danby talks to Dunera Boys."

30. Moore, *GI Jews*, 242.

31. Ann Marlowe, *David Galula: His Life and Intellectual Context* (Carlisle, PA: Strategic Studies Institute, US Army War College, 2010).

32. A. A. Cohen, *Galula: The Life and Writings of the French Officer Who Defined the Art of Counterinsurgency* (Santa Barbara, CA: ABC-CLIO [Praeger], 2012), 39.

33. Jean Caran, *The Tiger's Whiskers* (London: Walker, 1965).

34. Seymour Topping, *The Peking Letter: A Novel of the Chinese Civil War* (New York: Public Affairs, 1999).

35. Cohen, *Galula*, 21.

36. David Galula, *Counterinsurgency Warfare*. Santa Barbara, CA: Praeger, ([1964] 2006); David Galula, *Pacification in Algeria 1956–1958*. Santa Monica, CA: RAND Corporation ([1963], 2006). Also see the following article based on a report that Galula made for RAND in 1963: David Galula, "From Algeria to Iraq: All But Forgotten Lessons From Nearly 50 Years Ago," *RAND Review* 30, no. 2 (2006): 20–22.

37. US Army/Marine Corps, *Counterinsurgency Manual, US Army Field Manual 3-24; Marine Corps War Fighting Publication No. 3-33.5* (Chicago, IL: University of Chicago Press, 2007).

38. Ibid., 2-42.

39. See sources cited at end of: *Wikipedia*, s.v. "Operation Dragoon."

40. Jeffery J. Clarke and Robert Ross Smith, "HyperWar: Riviera to the Rhine," in *US Army in World War II, European Theater of Operations*, ed. Jeffrey J. Clark (Washington, DC: Office of the Chief of Military History, Department of the Army, 1993), 92, 122.

41. Ibid., 119.

42. Derek Ray Mallet, "Prisoners of War—Cold War Allies: The Anglo-American Relationship with Wehrmacht Generals" (a doctoral dissertation at Texas A&M University, 2009).

43. Elbert Hubbard, *A Message to Garcia* (Jason Liller, ed., Mechanicsburg, PA: Tremendous Life Books, [1899] 2002).

44. Harry Yeide and Mark Stout, *First to the Rhine: The Sixth Army Group in World War II* (St. Paul, MN: Zenith Press, 2007), 176.

45. Ibid., 192.

46. 191st Tank Battalion, *Commander's Narrative for the Month of October, 1944*, 4, Historical Paper Documents, National Archives and Records Administration, College Park, MD.

47. US Military Intelligence Service, "Recruitment of the Waffen-SS," Tactical and Technical Trends, No. 35 (October 7, 1943). Also see: Roger Cirillo, "Center of Military History Publication 72-26 Ardennes-Alsace: The US Army Campaigns of World War II," (Washington, DC: US Government Printing Office, 1995), 4.

48. Christopher R. Gabel, *The Lorraine Campaign: An Overview,*

September–December, 1944 (Ft. Leavenworth, KA: US Army Combat Studies Institute, 1985).

49. Statistical and Accounting Branch, Office of the US Adjutant General, *Army Battle Casualties and Nonbattle Deaths in World War II: Final Report, 7 December 1941–31, December, 1946* (1953).

50. US Defense Intelligence School, *Case Study (unclassified) of an Intelligence Failure: The Ardennes* (undated), 7. Provided to me by Denis Dwyer who had used this case study in a course in 1972.

51. Donald J. Hering, "134th Armored Ordnance Battalion," *Hellcat News* 59, No. 4, Ed. 1 (December, 2005), 11–12.

52. Harry Yeide, *Steel Victory: The Heroic Story of America's Independent Tank Battalions at War in Europe* (New York: Presidio, 2003), 12.

53. Yeide and Stout, *First to the Rhine*, 197.

54. Ibid., 198–199.

55. 191st Tank Battalion, *Commander's Narrative for the Month of October, 1944*, 4. Historical Paper Documents, National Archives and Records Administration, College Park, MD.

56. 191st Tank Battalion, *Commander's Narrative for the Month of November, 1944*, 4, Historical Paper Documents, National Archives and Records Administration, College Park, MD.

57. Ibid.

58. Ed Clark, "Mauldin's 45th Buddies Among First Into Reich," *Stars and Stripes* (1944), http://files.usgwarchives.net/ca/kern/newspapers/mauldins44gnw.txt.

59. 191st Tank Battalion, *Commander's Narrative for the Month of December, 1944*, 5, Historical Paper Documents, National Archives and Records Administration, College Park, MD.

60. US Defense Intelligence School, *Case Study (unclassified) of an Intelligence Failure: The Ardennes* (undated). Provided to me by Denis Dwyer who had used this case study in a course in 1972.

61. David P. Colley, *Decision at Strasbourg: Ike's Strategic Mistake to Halt the Sixth Army Group at the Rhine in 1944* (Annapolis, MD: Naval Institute Press, 2008).

62. 191st Tank Battalion, *Commander's Year End Report*, 7, Historical Paper Documents, National Archives and Records Administration, College Park, MD.

63. Wolf T. Zoepf, *Seven Days in January* (Bedford, PA: Aberjona Press, 2001), 68.

64. 191st Tank Battalion, *S-3 Journal, January 7, 1945* [Log of "Incidents, Messages, Orders, Etc."], Historical Paper Documents, National Archives and Records Administration, College Park, MD. ("S-3" is the designation for a battalion's operation and training officer who reports directly to the battalion commander. In the journal, "759376" refers to "wQ759376," a sector near Wingen-sur-Moder, France. The US Army used a mapping system called the "Nord de Guerre Grid." Its coordinates can be put into a conversion system and then shifted to Mapquest for viewing.)

65. Wallace Robert Cheves, *Battle of Wingen-sur-Moder: Operation Nordwind*, (Bennington, VT: Merriam Press, 2008); Charles Whiting. *The Other Battle of the Bulge: Operation Northwind* (Gloucester, England: Spellmount, 1988).

66. Zoepf, *Seven Days in January* (Bedford, PA: Aberjona Press, 2001).

67. Ibid., 106.

68. Ibid., 114–183.

69. 191st Tank Battalion, *S-3 Journal, January 3, 1945*.

70. Cheves, *Battle of Wingen-sur-Moder*, 43–44.

71. Zoepf, *Seven Days in January,* 156.

72. Ibid., 247.

73. Cheves, *Battle of Wingen-sur-Moder*, 178.

74. Ibid., 179.

75. Zoepf, *Seven Days in January,* 249.

76. Ibid., 262.

77. Ibid., 267.

78. Felix L. Sparks, *Dachau and Its Liberation* (website of the 45th Infantry Association and 157th Infantry Association, June 15, 1989).

79. Sparks description is supplemented by information from: Scrapbookpages website, www.scrapbookpages.com, s.v. "History of Dachau."

80. Bill Barrett, "Dachau Gives Answer To Why We Fought," *45th Division News*, V, no. 32, May 13, 1945).

81. Robert H. Abzug, *Inside the Vicious Heart: Americans and the Liberation of Nazi Concentration Camps* (New York: Oxford University Press, 1987).

82. US Army, *Military Awards, Army Regulation 600–8–22*, Sec. 2-8 Purple Heart (June 25, 2015), pages 21–26.

83. Veteran Tributes, "Top 50 Most Highly Decorated US Military Personnel of All Time," updated March 27, 2014.

84. Welborn G. Dolvin, unpublished farewell speech to 191st Tank Battalion, 1945 (document file-stamped February 6, 1947). Dave Kerr attachment to e-mail to Paul Levy, June 30, 2011.

85. *Wikipedia*, s.v. "World War II Casualties."

86. Stephen Daggett, "Costs of Major US Wars," Congressional Research Service, June 29, 2010.

87. Kurt Vonnegut, Jr., *Slaughterhouse Five or The Children's Crusade* (New York: Delacorte Press, 1969).

88. Modern Library, "100 Best Novels, The Board's List."

89. Clarke and Smith, *Hyperwar: Riviera to Rhine*, Chapter 27.

90. Roger Cirillo, "Center of Military History Publication 72-26 Ardennes-Alsace: The US Army Campaigns of World War II," (Washington, DC: US Government Printing Office, 1995), 51.

91. International Military Tribunal (Nuremberg), *Judgment of 1 October 1946*, 94.

92. Ibid., 94–95.

93. Richard Olafs Plavnieks, "'Wall of Blood:' The Baltic German Case Study in National Socialist Wartime Population Policy, 1939–1945," (a master of arts degree thesis, University of North Carolina, Chapel Hill, 2008), 12–13.

94. Domus Rigensis maintains a website and Facebook page in German and Latvian, s.v. "Domus Rigensis."

95. Keith E. Bonn, *When the Odds Were Even: The Vosges Mountains Campaign, October 1944–January 1945* (New York: Ballantine Books [1994], 2006).

96. Johann Voss, *Black Edelweiss: A Memoir of Combat and Conscience by a Soldier of the Waffen-SS* (Bedford, PA: Aberjona Press, 2002).

97. Johann Voss, "E-mail letter of June 18, 2011 to Paul Levy." My communication with Herr Voss was facilitated by Patti Bonn of Aberjona Press and began with an e-mail letter of June 14 from me to him.

98. Voss, *Black Edelweiss*, 2.

99. Ibid., 63.

100. John C. Wiley (US Envoy), "Letter to the Secretary of State on Anti-Semitism in Latvia, May 27, 1940."

101. US Military Intelligence Service, "Recruitment of the Waffen-SS," *Tactical and Technical Trends, No. 35* (October 7, 1943).

102. Jay Hatheway, *In Perfect Formation: SS-Ideology and the SS-Junkerschule-Tölz* (Atglen, PA: Schuiffer Military History Publications, 1999), 111–112.

103. *Jewish Virtual Library*, s.v. "The Waffen-SS."

104. Michael Sledge, *Soldier Dead: How We Recover, Identify, Bury, and Honor Our Military Fallen.* (New York: Columbia University Press, 2005), 23.

105. Edward Steere, "The Graves Registration Service in World War II, Q. M. C. Historical Studies, No. 21 (Washington, DC: US Government Printing Office, April, 1951), 1–15.

106. Sledge, *Soldier Dead*, 28.

107. Ibid., 67.

108. Quartermaster General of the US, *Tell Me About My Boy . . .* (1946), contained in the Collection of the US Army, Quartermaster Foundation, Ft. Lee, VA.

109. Margaret C. Colleran and Paul F. Colleran, *The Odyssey of 2d Lieutenant William J. Sheard: A Combat Officer in the G Company 157th Infantry Regiment of the 45th Infantry Division In World War II* (Needham, MA: Summerhill Press, 1999).

110. Edward Steere and Thayer M. Boardman, "Final Disposition of World War II Dead 1945–51," *QMC Historical Studies, Series II, No. 4* (Washington, DC: US Army, Quartermaster Corps, Historical Branch Office of the Quartermaster General, 1957), 671.

111. Ibid., 663, 686, 690.

112. 70th Division Association, *Trailblazer* 50, no. 91 (Winter, 1992), 6.

113. Mark Bando, *101st Airborne: The Screaming Eagles of World War II* (Osceola, WI: Zenith Press, 2007), Chapter 9.

114. John Russell, "Letter of August 15, 1996 to Wolf Zoepf." Shared by Denis Berger with Paul Levy.

115. Zoepf, *Seven Days in January*, 211, 242.

116. Ibid., 220.

117. *Jewish Virtual Library*, s.v. "The Waffen-SS."

Selected Bibliography

Bonn, Keith E. *When the Odds Were Even: The Vosges Mountains Campaign, October 1944–January 1945*. New York: Ballantine Books, 1994, 2006.

Cheves, Wallace Robert. *Battle of Wingen-sur-Moder: Operation Nordwind*. Bennington, VT: Merriam Press, 2008.

Cirillo, Roger. "Center of Military History Publication 72–76, Ardennes-Alsace: The US Army Campaigns of World War II." Washington, DC: US Government Printing Office, 1995.

Clarke, Jeffrey J., and Robert Ross Smith. "HyperWar: Riviera to the Rhine," In *US Army in World War II, European Theater of Operations*, ed. Jeffrey J. Clarke. Washington, DC: Office of the Chief of Military History, Department of the Army, 1993.

Cohen, A. A. *Galula: The Life and Writings of the French Officer Who Defined the Art of Counterinsurgency*. Santa Barbara, CA: ABC-CLIO (Praeger), 2012.

Colley, David P. *Decision at Strasbourg: Ike's Strategic Mistake to Halt the Sixth Army Group at the Rhine in 1944*. Annapolis, MD: Naval Institute Press, 2008.

Galula, David. *Counterinsurgency Warfare*. Santa Barbara, CA: Praeger, 2006. First published 1964.

Galula, David. *Pacification in Algeria 1956–1958*. Santa Monica, CA: RAND Corporation, 2006. First published 1963.

Grass, Günter. *Peeling the Onion*. NY: Harcourt Brace, 2006. English translation 2007.

Hatheway, Jay. *In Perfect Formation: SS-Ideology and the SS-Junkerschule-Tolz*. Atglen, PA: Schuiffer Military History Publications, 1999.

Lowry, Frank H. *Company A, 276th Infantry in World War II*. Self-published in Modesto, California, 1995.

Marlowe, Ann. *David Galula: His Life and Intellectual Context.* Carlisle, PA: Strategic Studies Institute, US Army War College, 2010.

Michie, Alan A. *Retreat to Victory.* Chicago, New York: Alliance Book Corp., 1942.

Moore, Deborah Dash. *GI Jews: How World War II Changed a Generation.* Cambridge, MA: Harvard University Press, 2004.

Quartermaster General of the United States 1946. *Tell Me About My Boy . . .* Contained in the Collection of the US Army, Quartermaster Foundation, Ft. Lee, VA.

Sledge, Michael. *Soldier Dead: How We Recover, Identify, Bury, and Honor Our Military Fallen.* New York: Columbia University Press, 2005.

US Army/Marine Corps. *Counterinsurgency Manual, US Army Field Manual 3-24; Marine Corps War Fighting Publication No. 3-33.5.* Chicago: University of Chicago Press, 2007.

Vonnegut, Kurt, Jr. *Slaughterhouse Five or The Children's Crusade.* New York: Delacorte Press, 1969.

Voss, Johann. *Black Edelweiss: A Memoir of Combat and Conscience by a Soldier of the Waffen-SS.* Bedford, PA: Aberjona Press, 2002.

Whiting, Charles. *The Other Battle of the Bulge: Operation Northwind.* Gloucester, England: Spellmount, 1988.

Yeide, Harry. *Steel Victory: The Heroic Story of America's Independent Tank Battalions at War in Europe.* New York: Presidio, 2003.

Yeide, Harry, and Mark Stout. *First to the Rhine: The Sixth Army Group in World War II.* St. Paul, MN: Zenith Press, 2007.

Zoepf, Wolf T. *Seven Days in January,* Bedford, PA: Aberjona Press, 2001.

Map and Photograph Credits

All maps by Jessica Ellis-Hopkins.
All photographs in France in 2014 by Elizabeth Levy, and except for the following listed images, the rest are from the author.

Page 36
Courtesy of the Northern Indiana Historical Society, Center for History, South Bend, Indiana.

Page 49
Courtesy of John Dziobko.

Page 60
Courtesy of British Armed Forces and National Service.
www.britisharmedforces.org

Page 74
—HM *Dunera* in Australia. Courtesy of National Archives of Australia and Migration Heritage Centre.
—Dunera Boys disembarking. Original source: Sydney Morning Herald, September 6, 1940.

Page 76
Courtesy of National Library of Australia and Migration Heritage Centre.

Pages 82, 83
Courtesy of Daniel Galula, with assistance of Alain A. Cohen, author of *Galula: The Life and Writings of the French Officer Who Defined the Art of Counterinsurgency*. Santa Barbara, CA: ABC-CLIO (Praeger), 2012.

Page 85
Imperial War Museum (photo by Official Navy Photographer, M.H.A. McNeill).

Page 91
Jeffrey J. Clarke and Robert Ross Smith. "HyperWar: Riviera to the Rhine," In *US Army in World War II, European Theater of Operations*, Jeffrey J. Clarke (ed.). Washington, DC: Office of the Chief of Military History, Department of the Army, 1993.

Page 101
Patton Museum of Calvary and Armor, Fort Knox, KY.

Pages 104, 119, 120, 124
Courtesy of 70th Infantry Division Association, Trailblazers website, www.Trailblazersww2.org (Steven Dixon, webmaster).

Pages 105
Courtesy of the National Archives and Records Administration, College Park, Maryland.

Pages 131–133
United States Holocaust Memorial Museum, courtesy of the National Archives and Records Administration, College Park, Maryland.

Page 145
Wolf T. Zoepf, *Seven Days in January*. Courtesy of Aberjona Press.

Page 146
Frank Lowry, *Company A 276th Infantry in World War II* (self-published). Courtesy of Teresa Scott, daughter of Frank Lowry.

Page 183
Courtesy of Olivier Lévy, published on Wikimedia.

Page 186
Courtesy of T. Sean Schulze and Eric Schell.

Acknowledgments

I am deeply indebted to many people who helped as I moved from initial queries to fragments of stories and eventually to publication.

I am very grateful to: my Aunt Jean (Phyllis Jean Levy Brown), Phil's younger sister, now deceased, for sharing memories, pictures, and letters of Phil; my Levy and Brown cousins for their support; Mark Van Aken, Phil's best friend in college, and Jack Del Monte (now deceased), a member of Phil's tank platoon, who provided memories of Phil; and Jane Josephson, Barbara's niece, who provided information and insights into Barbara's life.

I especially appreciate several people who helped me gather and understand military information: Dave Kerr, coordinator of the 45th Infantry Division Yahoo Group, who directed me to military record sources, explained such things as Allied map coordinates, and provided other help along the way; Denis Berger, a member of the 191st Tank Battalion and organizer of its past reunions and newsletters, who found valuable documents in his files and helped me understand various aspects of tank warfare; Sean Schulze and Eric Schell who walked the French-German border and shared their discoveries with the Yahoo Group and with me; and Mayor Jean Weisbecker and Linda and Jacky Bergmann who made my trip to France particularly memorable and who exhibit a deep French appreciation of American soldiers in World War II.

Many friends provided important editorial feedback and support: members of my writers group in Concord, New Hampshire, most notably Barbara Lassonde; professors Gil Schmerler and Gordon Pradl; authors Kay Kenady Sanger and her husband Tom; Tom White of the Cohen Center for Holocaust and Genocide Studies; historian Robert Ingalls; the poet/activist LR Berger; Nancy Wilson, Denis Dwyer, and Dan Dalberg. Helga Beatty and Barbara Barnett provided translation assistance. Others along the way provided important help: Patti Bonn, editor-in-chief of Aberjona Press, Johann Voss, Daniel Galula, Alain Cohen, and Karyn Driessen.

I feel very indebted to the friendly and talented folks at Bauhan Publishing—Sarah Bauhan, Mary Ann Faughnan, and Henry James. They made my foray into the publishing world particularly enjoyable and enlightening. I also especially appreciate Alice Fogel, New Hampshire's poet laureate and my editor, for her caring and valuable editorial work.

I owe several very special debts of gratitude. One is to my sister, Gail Levy Perlman. She has scrupulously edited each draft and been a wonderful dialogue partner in all matters related to the book. A second is to Jessica Ellis-Hopkins for preparing the book's important maps. And a third is to my wife Elizabeth who endured my four-year obsession with *Finding Phil* while managing to be tremendously supportive. She also helped edit and format an early, family edition of the book and served as photographer on our trip to France.